Aftereffects of Knowledge in Modernity

Aftereffects of Knowledge in Modernity

Politics, Aesthetics, and Individuality

Martin Leet

State University of New York Press

Published by
State University of New York Press, Albany

Printed in the United States of America

For information, address State University of New York Press,
90 State Street, Suite 700, Albany, NY 12207

Production by Michael Haggett
Marketing by Michael Campochiaro

Library of Congress Cataloging-in-Publication Data

Leet, Martin.
Aftereffects of knowledge in modernity : politics, aesthetics, and individuality / Martin Leet.
p. cm.
Includes bibliographical references and index.
ISBN 0-7914-6009-6 (alk. paper) — ISBN 0-7914-6010-X (pbk. : alk. paper)
1. Knowledge, Sociology of. 2. Knowledge, Theory of—Political aspects. 3. Individualism. 4. Progress. 5. Democracy. I. Title.

HM651.L44 2004
306.4'2—dc22

2004041606

10 9 8 7 6 5 4 3 2 1

Contents

Part II
Democracy, Aesthetics, and Individuality

Acknowledgments

Writing can seem like a solitary task, even though it involves a continuous dialogue with other writers. Fortunately, or unfortunately, none of the major theoretical protagonists in this book had a real chance to respond to my comments and criticisms. It was always only an echo that I heard in response to my questions and arguments, whether it was 'my Habermas' or 'my Nietzsche' or 'my Connolly'. I hope I have not made it too easy for myself by developing convenient interpretations.

For actual dialogue, in which critiques were more difficult to evade, I have a number of people to thank. Morgan Brigg, Richard Eckersley, Kate Feros, Dieter Freundlieb, Ian Hunter, Matt McDonald, Amanda Roan, Geoff Stokes, Barbara Sullivan, and Mark Warren contributed useful feedback on various chapters. I always received a wealth of commentary from April Carter. Di Zetlin must be happy that I have seen the error of my theoretical ways although I resist admitting that she is right. I owe a special thanks to Roland Bleiker who encouraged me to keep going. The analysis of the entire manuscript by the anonymous reviewer at SUNY Press helped me to sharpen things up a great deal.

Paul Boreham, as head of the School of Political Science and International Studies at the University of Queensland, has been generous in providing institutional support. The kind and efficient administrative staff of the school, especially Ros Nicol, assisted with many of the logistical tasks associated with writing. Thanks go to Chris for being supportive throughout. Finally, I am grateful to my family for their encouragement of my philosophical wanderings.

Earlier versions of some of these chapters have been published as journal articles. Chapter 1 originally appeared as "Recovering the Individual: Subjectivity or Intersubjectivity as a Framework for Critical Theory?" *Contemporary Political Theory* 1, no. 1 (2002), 19–38 and is reproduced with permission of Palgrave Macmillan; chapter 2 draws on "The Politics of Suffering: Progress, Modernity and the Adolescent Crisis," *Australian Journal of Political Science* 37, no. 1 (2002), 7–20 and is reprinted with permission of Taylor and Francis (http://www.tandf.co.uk); chapter 3 appeared as "Aftereffects of Knowledge: Dogmatic Retreats and Sceptical Adventures," *Critical Horizons* 3, no. 2 (2002), 201–223 and is reproduced with permission of Brill Academic Publishers; and parts of chapters 4 and 5 draw on material that first appeared as "Democracy and the Individual—Deliberative and Existential Negotiations," *Philosophy and Social Criticism* 29, no. 6 (2003) and is reprinted with permission of Sage Publications.

It is very unhappy, but too late to be helped, the discovery we have made that we exist. That discovery is called the Fall of Man. Ever afterwards we suspect our instruments. We have learned that we do not see directly, but mediately, and that we have no means of correcting these colored and distorting lenses which we are, or of computing the amount of their errors.

—Ralph Waldo Emerson

The falseness of a judgment is to us not necessarily an objection to a judgment: it is here that our new language perhaps sounds strangest.

—Friedrich Nietzsche

Introduction

What Is the Value of Knowledge?

Knowledge and the relentless accumulation of knowledge are defining features of modern life. The inhabitants of Western civilization, in particular, stand out in the history of humankind in terms of how much they know about the world and about themselves. And no matter how far and wide our knowledge extends, the drive to knowledge, the tenacious will to know persists. What are the consequences of this individual and collective gathering of knowledge? What does all this curiosity mean?

This book is concerned with what Nietzsche once called the "aftereffects of knowledge."[1] These aftereffects are ambiguous. Knowledge has advantages and disadvantages, it can be helpful but it can also make life more complicated. In earlier phases of the modern project of enlightenment, the advantages tended to be emphasized. Rational knowledge was understood as the key to human emancipation and fulfillment. Many intellectuals still hold this belief about the role of knowledge. They do so not only out of self-interest. There are good reasons for believing in the positive power of knowledge since numerous cognitive advances have alleviated a great deal of human suffering. Knowledge has indeed proven to be an important source of material freedom and happiness as we have increased our understanding of, and power over, life and the world. The prospect of an increasing mass of objective and universally recognized knowledge holds out the possibility that we will, together, advance along the path to a better and better future.

But the darker sides of knowledge have also been made apparent, especially so in recent times. We have, with the means of knowledge, come to see how the drive to knowledge itself can be a very destructive force. Public consciousness is increasingly aware of this questionable dimension to knowledge-seeking as it learns of a proliferating number of depressing scenarios about the future environmental, biological, and social conditions of life. Humans could not have made earthly existence so precarious without extensive knowledge. What is required to address these problems, suggest some, is a refined knowledge in other areas such as ethics and politics. With understanding in these dimensions, they say, we will be in a position to apply science in ways that are more humane and peaceful. The doubts about knowledge are now deep enough, however, to cast suspicion on such recommendations. The desire for more complete forms of knowledge may, indeed, be particularly dangerous. What, then, is the value of knowledge?

Anthony Giddens characterizes our present predicament in terms of the concept "manufactured uncertainty," since many problems no longer lead from a lack of human power over inimical natural or social forces but from the byproducts of the exercise of this very power. The differences between knowledge and social reality, in his view, have become blurred insofar as reality itself is determined further and further by the application of knowledge. Giddens explains:

> Manufactured risk is a result *of* human intervention into nature and into the conditions of social life. The uncertainties (and opportunities) it creates are largely new. They cannot be dealt with by age-old remedies; but neither do they respond to the Enlightenment prescription: more knowledge, more control. Put more accurately, the sorts of reaction we might make to them today are often as much about "damage control" and "repair" as about an endless process of increasing mastery.[2]

More intellectual enquiry, therefore, may not lead to a clear and sound basis for action but to ever greater degrees of uncertainty.

Apart from these factors of uncertainty, there is also a question about the desirability of the knowledge we amass. The issue of palatability emerges especially with regard to the knowledge we gain about ourselves—we may not like what we find. Enhanced levels of self-understanding, particularly with regard to the ethical and political dimensions of existence, could prove more disabling than liberating. Wendy Brown has written about how an increasingly reflective form of progressive politics tends to extend its awareness beyond external resistance to its ambitions for a better world and bring into focus the substantial contradictions from within. She demonstrates how "ostensibly emancipatory or democratic political projects" can often "problematically mirror the mechanisms and configurations of power of which they are an effect and which they purport to oppose."[3] Similarly, Romand Coles asks whether there might be "something about generosity," an internal paradox, a "forgetting" that "turns [it] away from the spirit of the project entirely and tends rather in directions of pillage and death?"[4] The addition of layer after layer of knowledge, in other words, can produce a sense of confusion and horror at the unanticipated consequences of action as well as deep-seated doubt about the real nature of one's intentions. Might ignorance now be a value worth defending against the will to know, if lack of insight could make thought and action less difficult? Besides, can we *know* anything at all?

The focus of this book is on the consequences for politics and ethics of these tendencies for knowledge to undermine itself and destabilize our orientation in the world. In particular, it considers the turn to individuality these contradictions of knowledge-seeking appear to bring about. For the modern confidence in knowledge has often relied on a lack of awareness about its underlying presuppositions and motives. We are now invited, and in many ways forced, to become more self-reflective, to uncover and understand those hopes and fears which have led us to value knowledge to begin with. Significantly, this "return to ourselves" gives us reason to question the *collective* dimension of progressive politics. For when the nexus between knowledge and progress is broken, what can possibly tie us together in a shared understanding and vision of the future? Without a sure footing in universal and objective knowledge, a collective approach to progressive politics is exposed as no less forceful and oppressive than that which it seeks to overcome. We can no longer project, in good conscience, our merely individual desires and doubts onto a collective struggle that aims at a better political future for everyone. Rather, we need to recognize and come to grips with those forces and attractions that first led us away from our individual selves toward a mirage of organized omniscience.

It will be argued in this book that the renewed focus on the individual evident in certain parts of progressive theory is a necessary and desirable one. Potentially, though, such a focus is also politically dangerous. To begin with, it is still both reasonable and necessary for many social and political problems to be collectively and democratically managed. Individuals depend, for their well-being, on forms of social, economic, and cultural infrastructure which they are unable to reproduce by themselves. Second, the dominance in public debates of a range of conservative discourses of individuality makes it difficult and perhaps strategically undesirable to enter such biased terms of discussion. The introduction of individualist themes, even with good intentions, can play into a politics of blame and mean-spiritedness in which the already disadvantaged are held responsible for their life-conditions. Finally, the philosophical and practical dimensions of arts of self-cultivation that ensue from a return to the individual may, in themselves, contain antipolitical biases that render them unhelpful for progressive struggles. It could be the case, as Socrates contends, that the "true champion of justice, if he intends to survive even for a short time, must necessarily confine himself to private life and leave politics alone."[5] This ambivalence about individuality in parts of the contemporary political-theoretical landscape—about its importance for and tension with progressive politics—is the subject of this book.

The remainder of this introductory chapter sets out the general context in which these themes will be discussed. It reconstructs two general stories about knowledge and its political and ethical aftereffects. The first story is about an attempt to justify a revised faith in knowledge. It emphasizes the need to provide ethics and politics with foundations in knowledge, a need that, for many, must be urgently addressed precisely as a result of the corrosive effects of the search for knowledge itself. It is important to note that this story tends to ignore or suppress the dimension of individuality in its narrative about progressive politics. It suggests such individualist concerns cannot be treated in a rational, universal, and, therefore, collective fashion, meaning any attempt to pursue them will only play into the hands of those who wish to abandon the project of modernity. Throughout the book, Jürgen Habermas represents this story about the aftereffects of knowledge and the first part constitutes a sustained critique of his views. The second story, on the other hand, articulates the importance of human needs and desires other than cognitive justification in the pursuit and application of knowledge. It suggests progressive politics requires individuals to engage in certain practices of self-cultivation if the ambitions of a better world are to be realized. The nature and importance of such practices will be examined throughout this book in relation to a number of writers and traditions, including Friedrich Nietzsche, Ralph Waldo Emerson, Max Weber, various aspects of ancient Greek thought, and the more recent contributions of George Kateb, and William Connolly. The focus will be on how these theorists have conceived of the relations between politics and individuality in order to draw out some conclusions about the compatibility of these often competing ideals.

Two Stories About the Aftereffects of Knowledge

Thousands of years ago, a philosopher formed some rather deep-ranging doubts about knowledge. After years of searching, in vain, for the truth about the cosmos, Socrates confessed his endless ignorance. In response to this failure to reach any definitive conclusions about the material world of the universe, he turned his attention to basic, practical questions of how to live. As Cornford explains, the Socratic philosophy gave up on the search for knowledge of "material substance in external Nature and turn[ed] its eyes inwards to the nature of the human soul. This was the revolution accomplished by Socrates, with his Delphic injunction 'Know thyself.'"[6] But this shift inward seemed also to be fruitless. Even in respect of the art of living, Socrates admitted to being "barren and sterile in wisdom." In his words, "I ask questions of others, but find no answers of my own to those questions because I have no wisdom."[7] Socrates' life and philosophy are paradoxical. He insists that right action and happiness can only be based in genuine and valid knowledge. And while he seemed to know how to act correctly in even difficult situations, Socrates is adamant that he knows nothing at all. This Socratic paradox may be insoluble. I have mentioned it only because, as noted above, more recent developments in philosophical discourse have focused on similar problems. The challenge of living ethically while being radically skeptical imposes itself on a modern consciousness increasingly aware of the limits of knowledge. Two general stories about this deepening form of self-reflection are considered here as possible responses to this challenge.

The early stages of the modern enlightenment, as already discussed, were supported by the belief that the achievement of cognitive certainty would enable increasing control over the natural and social worlds in the service of noble human aspirations. For the first time in history, so the story goes, morality, justice, and happiness might be established on a collective scale. The logic and dynamics of modern economies and societies still express this view, oriented as they are around the systematic application of knowledge. At a philosophical and cultural level, however, there has emerged the kind of doubts considered earlier, doubts about a knowledge-driven approach to progress. The arrival of a "postmodern" outlook and sensibility has placed a question mark next to the claim that we will be able to reach our goals via a search for secure knowledge. In the words of Zygmunt Bauman,

> It is perhaps debatable whether the philosophers of the modern era ever articulated to everybody's satisfaction the foundations of the objective superiority of Western rationality, logic, morality, aesthetics, cultural precepts, rules of civilized life, etc. The fact is, however, that they never stopped looking for such an articulation and hardly ever ceased to believe that the search would bring—must bring—success. The post-modern period is distinguished by abandoning the search itself, having convinced itself of its futility. Instead, it tries to reconcile itself to a life under conditions of permanent and incurable uncertainty; a life in the presence of an unlimited quantity of competing forms of life, unable to prove their claims to be grounded in anything more solid and binding than their own historically shaped conventions.[8]

The failure to find the foundations of modernity in objective knowledge is, nevertheless, not fatal to the project of enlightenment. Indeed, for narrators of the first story examined here, it is a rather feeble objection since the better formulations of this project have always relied on a "nonobjective" conception of knowledge and action. Not unlike Socrates' turn to practice and ethics, Kant's "turn to the subject" made clear that the modern search for knowledge should be a self-critical one. The form of criticism and knowledge-seeking that Bauman and others have objected to, as the root cause of modernity's violence, is one that tends to condemn existing reality in contrast to an ideal image of society and politics. Connerton calls this "critique as oppositional thinking."[9] The idea of critique to be found in the tradition of critical theory, on the other hand, has its roots in Kant. Kant introduced this mode of critique in the context of debates between the "empiricists" and "dogmatists" of his time. He observed that both parties assumed the world can be known as it really is, as a "thing-in-itself." The only difference of importance, from the point of view of such debates, is whether the "thing-in-itself" is empirical or metaphysical. Kant maintained, to the contrary, that each party ignored the fact that knowledge is dependent on and first made possible by the "knowing subject." He argued that to understand what knowledge is, we must begin by reflecting on its general, necessary, and unavoidable *preconditions*. Alternatively, to focus on what we think we know perpetuates an ignorance of the process via which the object of knowledge is initially constituted. In historical terms, according to Habermas, "Kantian philosophy marks the birth of a new mode of justification."[10]

The critique of critical theory, then, does not separate itself from the object of criticism as though the two move in completely different universes. Before playing any role in affecting beliefs or institutional practices, the first task of critique is to understand its own place *within* those beliefs and practices. Following Horkheimer's differentiation of "traditional" from "critical theory,"[11] Benhabib argues that since "theoretical activity [i]s a moment in the general life of society, for critical theorists, how, under which conditions, and to what ends theory enters social praxis is a question that they pose themselves."[12] Properly understood, critique is a reflection of knowledge or reason on itself rather than a juxtaposition of knowledge and society. Critique attempts to remain immanent within the social process rather than proclaim that it has a neutral standpoint in the outside or beyond.

Critical theorists think it is very important that critique and knowledge do not become "premature" as it were, that they remain modest and contained within their limits. Given this motivation, a number of variations on Kant's theoretical "move" or reflective "turn" have been developed in an attempt to sustain the immanence of critical knowledge. Thus, while Kant's substantive account may be rejected, the idea that the proper focus of philosophy and theory is to look behind and before our knowledge, experience and action has been consistently endorsed. Indeed, the basic idea is extended to look at preconditions that lie beyond the subject, in the broader social and political dimensions of existence. We hear, then, of "social," "linguistic," "interpretive," "pragmatic," and "communicative" turns. Kant's knowing subject has been swamped by transsubjective phenomena in an ongoing "Copernican Revolution."

Nonetheless, this narrative about the aftereffects of knowledge in modernity remains deeply committed to the earlier aspirations of enlightenment, even while its modes of self-limitation and awareness become ever more sophisticated and ingenuous. Such a commitment must persist as long as critique and knowledge are still connected to the intention of justification. *This* search for knowledge, however complex it becomes, remains a search for certainty. Contemporary critical theorists like Jürgen Habermas persevere in tying critique with justification. It is still assumed that theory and practice require a grounding in universally valid forms of knowledge. Even if this knowledge is supposed to be of a nonobjective kind, the underlying motives and aspirations are continuous with objectivism. For Habermas, the search for a *rational* orientation in the context of unprecedented levels of contingency and uncertainty is the defining philosophical theme of modernity. "As modernity awakens to consciousness of itself," he says, as it realizes the implications of its break from all past traditions and standards, "a need for self-reassurance arises."[13] Habermas agrees with Hegel that the contemporary history of modernity has been elevated to "the rank of philosophy"[14] since it is a time and place that seeks to stabilize itself on the basis of reason rather than with reference to unjustified principles.

> Modernity can and will no longer borrow the criteria by which it takes its orientation from the models supplied by another epoch; *it has to create its normativity out of itself.* Modernity sees itself cast back upon itself without any possibility of escape. This explains the sensitiveness of its self-understanding, the dynamism of the attempt, carried forward incessantly down to our time, to "pin itself down."[15]

Habermas argues the search for rational foundations must not be abandoned and he believes, in fact, that he has culled the right answer from the mass of human enquiry. The "communicative concept of reason" in his view can fulfill, in an enlightened way, integrative functions of the kind previously satisfied by myth and religion. For him, this communicative rationality is the solution various protagonists of the philosophical discourse of modernity have searched for in vain because of their inability to break free from the "philosophy of the subject."

Is this search for foundations sustainable? For, on the one hand, the tendency is to pursue knowledge as the necessary condition of thought and action. And yet, as discussed earlier, the very pursuit of knowledge itself tends to be disabling as doubts and uncertainties proliferate rather than dissolve. While immanent and self-reflective critique presents itself as a convincing way out of this contradiction, must it not prove ultimately unsuccessful since it merely refashions rather than displaces the pursuit of authoritative knowledge? Does it not merely add to the complexity and confusion that are part and parcel of the accumulation of knowledge? Or is it the case, as Habermas and others would like to argue, that it is not logically possible to displace the attempt to justify? Could we ever be as ironical and paradoxical as Socrates?

The sublimation of the search for certain knowledge from the outer to the inner is not the only story about the aftereffects of knowledge. The elements of a different narrative have been emerging in more recent discussions, as explorations are being made into the consequences of accepting the fruitlessness of such a search. Here, the turn inward is separated from motives of cognitive justification. In this connection, Stephen White has spoken of a "weak-ontological turn."[16] The idea of weak ontology responds to the failure of previous "turns" to come fully to grips with the fallibility of knowledge while still aiming to provide ethical and political orientation. White tells a story something like the following. He notes, to begin, that in past epochs, comprehensive ontological and metaphysical conceptions of self and world provided relatively clear guidelines for individual and collective action. Some conservative critics of modernity argue we need to return to this "strong ontological" mode of thinking. The kind of modernist political theory considered above, by contrast, insists that such thinking is neither applicable nor desirable in what is now a "postmetaphysical" age. The quest for incontestable foundations is to sustain itself via a thinning-out strategy in which the diversity of thick ontological notions are reduced to a common denominator. The formal proceduralism of political liberalism, to be found in figures such as Habermas and Rawls, is the usual result of this thinning-out approach.

Meanwhile, postmodernists and poststructuralists tend to be relentless in their critique and unmasking of the potential for oppression and exclusion lurking in all foundational conceptions. They contest political liberalism precisely at the point where it upholds the pursuit of certainty. As White argues, though, these theorists, guided by such negative and destructive imperatives, have great difficulty in providing a coherent ethical-political orientation. And if we are looking for such an orientation, but it is clear that strong ontology is out of the question under present circumstances, we may necessarily become disappointed and rather disoriented if there is only a choice between postmodern negativity and a thin, almost contentless political liberalism.

White provides an overview and defense of a different way of doing political theory. He contends that if we do not begin with the assumption that incontestable foundations are required, then we can bypass the endless and rather debilitating debates over questions of justification. If we concede, also, that thick ontological conceptions simply cannot be avoided, then we are in a better position to employ such conceptions in a self-consciously critical manner. "Weak ontology," White claims, provides a substantial form of ethical and political orientation without falling into fundamentalist traps. He argues there are four central characteristics of this approach.[17] First, there is a recognition that ontological conceptualizations are indispensable features of ethical and political life, even while they are contestable in nature. In this respect, White aims to shift the intellectual burden of proof away from those who use ontological ideas, faced as they are by an array of critics all too ready to deconstruct and criticize. But he insists that the contestability of such ideas must not only be announced but "enacted" or "performed" if weak ontologies are not to slide into strong ontological terrain. Second, weak ontologies do not *begin* with ontological ideas but offer "figurations of human being" in response to a set of existential issues with which we must all contend. Connected with this is a third characteristic: since responding to existential issues is the primary motive of weak ontologies, rather than theoretical justification as such, they are also concerned with what White calls "cultivation." In a way similar to traditional ideas about cultivating virtues, weak ontologies offer affective as well as cognitive orientation. They shape and modify our sensibilities, aiming to help us "cope with the pressures and challenges of late modern life." Fourth, weak ontologies point to the importance of another aspect of the relationship between theory and practice. Compared to strong ontologies which "determine" our ethics and politics, weak ontologies merely "prefigure" judgment and action. The relationships between the level of prefiguration, sensibility, and specific contexts of application are open to constant feedback and revision.

This brief account of a second understanding of the aftereffects of knowledge points to the contestability of the meaning of "knowledge" itself. As Barbara Herrnstein Smith explains, the

> beliefs of individuals are traditionally conceived as sets of either discrete, true/false mental *propositions* about the world or discrete, correct/incorrect interior *representations* of it. Beliefs may be reconceived, however, as *configurations of linked perceptual/behavioral tendencies* of various *degrees* of strength, continuously formed, transformed, and reconfigured through our ongoing interactions with our environments. That is, rather than sentences about, or pictures of, an *outside* world located *inside* the organism's mind, brain, or body and motivating its actions accordingly, what we call beliefs could be seen as the *entire* organism's complexly linked—and continuously shifting, growing, weakening, and recombining—tendencies to perceive and act in the world in certain ways.[18]

This idea of knowledge as bound up with the individual's entire mode of being helps make sense of the claim, put forward by Bennett, that there can be "no ethics without aesthetics."[19] That is, ethics understood as a code or set of principles must remain ineffective and contradictory without attention being paid to dispositions and sensibilities. If the affective levels of being remain undisciplined and untutored, then the adoption of abstract rules will merely act as a noble mask, a mask usually exposed in practice by the mean and miserly application of formal rules. Aesthetic practices, in Bennett's view, make a more genuine and spirited ethics possible because they work on the dimension of sensibility and extend "the range of possibility in perception, enactment, and responsiveness to others."[20]

As will be indicated in the following chapters, this way of thinking about ethical and political theory is not all that recent. A number of authors have emphasized how such modes of theory and practice stretch back to the various schools of ancient philosophy, providing interesting contrasts with many modern approaches.[21] Nehamas asserts that modern thinkers such as Montaigne, Nietzsche, and Foucault, in their encounters with the ancients generally and Socrates in particular, have recapitulated an "inward turn."[22] Ian Hunter has argued this approach to the history of philosophy can be used to reinterpret even those thinkers who explicitly resist such a conception.[23] Along these lines, he advances a major reinterpretation of Kant, and Kantianism more generally.[24] For him, Wittgenstein's dictum that "work in philosophy . . . is really more work on oneself" holds true.[25] Like White, he maintains that anthropologies, psychologies, and cosmologies are to be seen not as "quasi-scientific theories of the subject or the cosmos" but as "reflexive ethical instruments," as "modes of fashioning persons for envisaged circumstances."[26] From this point of view, theories are the vehicle

> through which the members of specific intellectual elites acquire the capacity to take up a particular relation to themselves and their world. This is typically a relation that imbues such individuals with a conviction of their deviation from an ideal way of thought or life—a relation of self-problematization. In this way they are inducted into a particular intellectual regimen or practice of self-cultivation, through which they may reshape themselves in the image of this ideal.[27]

Knowledge, Aesthetics, and Individuality

What is knowledge? If knowledge is thought to be propositional and representational in kind, the interesting theoretical question becomes one of how many correct beliefs can be accumulated on a collective scale. This approach is found in the narratives of writers like Weber and Habermas with their theories of modern rationalization. Alternatively, if knowledge is understood as only one moment of dynamic processes of perception and behavior, then a psychology and physiology of the individual moves to the foreground. Here, we may become less interested in the correctness of beliefs and more curious about why we want beliefs at all. It is at this point, in recent political theory, that questions of *aesthetics* have been raised. In this section of the chapter, I would like to clarify the significance of this important theme of contemporary discussions in the context of the two stories told above.

One way of considering the role and place of the aesthetic is in terms of its relationship to the cognitive and moral dimensions of knowledge. Weber and Habermas suggest that before the onset of modern processes of rationalization, the cognitive, moral and aesthetic spheres of cultural value were relatively unified. In the structures of traditional societies, they say, truth, goodness, and beauty reciprocally defined one another in the context of an overarching worldview. The cognitive pursuit of knowledge was molded by clear moral beliefs and the requirements of morality itself could be ascertained by correct knowledge of the world. Aesthetic appreciation played an important role in moral edification and was also enlisted in the service of portraying cognitive truths. The unifying power of worldviews broke down as these three spheres of value began to pursue their "own inner logics." The cognitive pursuit of knowledge took less and less into account its moral and aesthetic implications; moral questions now had to be answered without the guidance of ethically laden natural and social structures; and the aesthetic realm of taste and beauty sought to free itself from cognitive and moral influences.

The sociological level of analysis Habermas adopts from Weber leads him to see the importance of differentiating between the cognitive, moral, and aesthetic. Habermas emphasizes separateness because it appears to be a condition of possibility for a democratic and pluralist culture. He thus compares the openness of modern societies with the rigidity of traditional societies in terms of the degree of differentiation of the three spheres of value.[28] A great potential for learning arises, in his view, when human inquiry and activity is freed from the restrictions and taboos of a social order structured in correspondence with a fixed metaphysical worldview. When each sphere or dimension of knowledge is freed from the demands of the others, it can be allowed to develop autonomously and accumulate beliefs and understanding on its own terms. The process of "decentration" leaves individuals with only *formal* standards of evaluation, allowing them a degree of independence with regard to specific beliefs, beliefs that were not even recognized as mere beliefs in premodern worldviews.

Important for the present discussion is a key aim of Habermas's particular account of modern rationalization: to contest Weber's view that the differentiation of value spheres inevitably leaves behind only the cognitive dimension of rationality, largely excluding moral and aesthetic ideals from modern social and political life. Habermas seeks to develop a more open-ended and balanced understanding of modern development by allowing for the possibility of rationalization processes in all three spheres of value, not just in the cognitive realm. He also hopes to show that while remaining differentiated, the three spheres can be linked in provisional and constructive ways and therefore forestall a loss of meaning. Once again, Habermas is seeking to overcome the prejudices of the philosophy of the subject and its tendency to narrow down our experience with instrumentalist attitudes and restrict our range of beliefs to those concerning "states of affairs." Yet, I wonder whether his model is as open-ended and encompassing as he would like us to believe.

Habermas's approach is itself prejudiced, I would argue, precisely because it looks at things from the point of view of rationalization. In adopting unproblematically Weber's general concept of rationalization, Habermas makes his problem and task one of demonstrating that the moral and aesthetic spheres are indeed capable of rationalization processes. He hopes to show that these forms of knowledge are valuable and significant because they *can* be "rendered cumulative," they *can* be institutionalized in "reflective learning processes," and they *can*, therefore, have a "structure-forming effect on society as a whole."[29] But is this what we want from morality and aesthetics? Should we aim to "rationalize" in these areas?[30]

The aesthetic has featured in recent discussions as a rubric under which precisely this demand for rationalization can be contested. The aesthetic signifies forms of nonrationalizable theory and practice that need to be preserved and protected against the onslaught of propositional and representational knowledge. Romand Coles argues, for example, that Habermas's theory is insensitive to the aesthetic because it overvalues the importance of agreement and the need to develop widely acceptable forms of knowledge in social life. Reading Habermas, he says, we get the impression there is a relentless "pressure to adapt" built into the very conditions of human life that makes it crucial for human beings to agree about appropriate courses of action. Individuals exist "under conditions of finitude and scarcity" and so meaning that is identical for participants in interaction is vital "in order to facilitate the speedy and precise coordination of complex interactions."[31] Even with the move from action to discourse, which Habermas says suspends the pressures of everyday life, the compulsion to agree and adapt in response to intersubjective uncertainty maintains the telos of consensus as the defining principle and motivation. In Coles's words, "like an overly flexed muscle or a muscle formed through a singular kind of flexing, the structure of the pressurized 'normal' defines the operation."[32]

From the point of view of Habermas's theory, then, the world tends to exist only in relation to the demands and inhibitions of a machinelike rationalization process. But why should we restrict knowledge and understanding to domains capable of "structure-forming" effects? Why is Habermas not very interested in those forms of perception and insight that work against reducing the world to human proportions? Should we not be concerned with learning how to relieve and relax those pressures of cutting the world down to the size and shape of human fears, needs, and desires? Coles maintains, following Adorno, that critical theory must aim at "increasing our consciousness of the world's otherness" as opposed to legitimating metaphysical presumptions that construct the world as it exists *for us*.[33] Martin Morris also draws on Adorno in his critique of Habermas and adds to the chorus calling for a renewed emphasis on an aesthetic sensibility as a way of "foster[ing] a non-instrumental concern for and relationship to others, a new compassion or passionate care that could be universalizable."[34]

As it is used in this book, the aesthetic has both a "methodological" and a "substantive" meaning. Methodologically, it involves a theoretical obligation to pay attention to the layers of sensibility formation. In this respect, it is about the return to the individual. It is a recognition of the importance of practices of self-cultivation as both always already in existence and in need of conscious attention by those concerned with political change. Substantively, the aesthetic has an ethical significance insofar as it calls for a specific kind of mindfulness about the inherent violence of human thought and action. Because aesthetic approaches "assume that there is always a gap between a form of representation and what is represented therewith"[35] they are useful in contesting the dogmatism of entrenched worldviews. Morton Schoolman has brought these two aspects together in his clarification of the links between aesthetics and individuality. Schoolman argues that the aesthetic refers to a kind of openness and responsiveness that contrasts sharply with those tendencies in the modern world toward control and the repression of difference. He distinguishes "formal reason" that "finds what is unknown and different from thought to be an obstacle to its emancipation from fear" from an "aesthetic reason" that is "unafraid of the unfathomable in which it finds the source of its receptivity to the diversity of different forms of life."[36] This aesthetic mode of relating to the world is, in turn, essential to individuality because it is a way of resisting the tendency of thought to identify itself with the object of thought and thereby produce conformity. The development of an aesthetic sensibility that is aware of the inadequacy of all representations of the world, in other words, is a condition of possibility of individuality because it protects one from becoming a pale imitation of dominant ideas and influences.

Habermas believes his communicative paradigm, in which the aesthetic is given a place among the other dimensions of rationality, is the better solution to the violent and repressive tendencies of modernity. The argument developed in this book, by contrast, is that it is precisely such a domestication of the aesthetic and, in turn, the individual which is complicit with modern processes of subjugation. It is the collective and cognitive biases of Habermas's intersubjective theoretical orientation that places such an exaggerated emphasis on the need for differentiation between the three spheres of rationality and on the value of rationalization. Quite obviously, social structures organized around a nonmodern metaphysical principle violate the conditions of modern pluralism and modern rational learning. Nevertheless, as will be elaborated further throughout the first part of this book, Habermas's conception of differentiation itself expresses a metaphysics, a metaphysics that reflects and endorses a society organized around attaining more and more knowledge and control. Since language takes center stage in this approach, the inner world of subjectivity can be displaced to the periphery along with its link to the aesthetic. From other perspectives, though, the aftereffects of knowledge deny language its function as a kind of "protective net," obstructing a turn to the individual. The final chapter, in particular, will indicate how these other points of view, in which individuality as a world of embodied consciousness is central, offer a very different understanding of the meanings of and relationships between the cognitive, moral, and aesthetic domains.

Politics and Individuality

If our cognitive expectations about knowledge have dimmed and we can see that only practices of self-cultivation give knowledge its significance, then a return to the individual seems compelling. Individuals need to work on themselves in order to make the social environment more hospitable to values like pluralism, equality, and democracy. Formal institutions and organizations obtain results but only by having built into them a pressurized logic that inhibits thought and action. Individuals are, in principle, more able to cultivate modes of being attuned to a recognition of the world less discolored by all-too-human fears and desires. In thinking about the relations between politics, aesthetics, and individuality, the hope is that such sensibilities can infiltrate and modify the hardened structures of living characteristic of modern existence.

As mentioned earlier, however, such a return to the individual is a potentially dangerous one for progressive politics. Public discourses of individuality tend to be constructed in accordance with conservative agendas of reform. Concepts like personal responsibility and individual character are often used in order to erase the collective dimensions of social and economic problems. Emphasis on these themes may serve to justify a retreat of government from regulating and modifying unequal relations of power. This vision is not pluralist and democratic, rather it is administratively manufactured and implemented. Individuality is systematically truncated because it comes to mean conformity to collectively imposed norms and standards.

"Third way" politicians and theorists have slipped easily into these discourses of inhibited individuality. The third way is supposed to be about constructing a social democratic reformism beyond traditional distinctions between left and right. While many on the left agree that old dogmas need to be radically revised, the theorists of the third way appear to have been unable to adopt a distinctive discourse of individuality able to avoid the stinginess and lack of generosity characteristic of their political opponents. The emphases on neoliberal economics and conservative social virtues discourage resistance to the existing social and political order and capitulate to those modes of individual development already sanctioned. The third way promotes work on oneself that entrenches rather than questions restrictive sensibilities and orientations.[37]

At the present time, then, it is politically risky for progressives to emphasize the importance of individuality. Public debate is already overcrowded with discourses of economic individualism that define the terms of discussion and distort the nature of the possible alternatives. But if individuality is important, as will be argued here, then we would be irresponsible to ignore it. A number of questions then arise: If we are to take up these themes, how should we do so? Can practices of self-cultivation be placed in political contexts? What role is there for the political understood as a concern for the common and general? The second part of this book focuses on the issues raised in response to these and other questions as they are manifested in discussions about democracy in contemporary political theory. It considers various attempts to extend democracy in an effort to understand whether and how such attempts need to incorporate themes of individuality. In order to contextualize the discussion at this point, I would like to consider briefly a few theses developed by Richard Rorty. For Rorty's reflections on democracy represent a unique combination of the first and second stories about the aftereffects of knowledge discussed above. These reflections are both a recognition and displacement of the importance of individuality. And because they house conflicting views, they tend to provoke a great deal of critical attention that highlights alternative understandings of the relations between politics, aesthetics, and individuality.

To begin, Rorty subscribes to the second story about knowledge and its aftereffects insofar as he believes the need for cognitive reassurance, articulated by theorists like Habermas, is a false one. It is a "psychological problem," he says, "found only within the souls of bourgeois liberals who have not yet gone postmodern, the ones who are still using the rationalist rhetoric of the Enlightenment to back up their liberal ideas."[38] Rorty suggests a link between morality, on the one hand, and a willingness to resign from efforts of philosophical justification, on the other hand. He adopts the view that a concern for truth is linked to a subtle violence. And he advocates a "Deweyian culture" in which we are to we leave behind "an ambition of transcendence" and rely only on our historically formed intuitions.[39] This strategy sounds disturbing to theorists like Habermas who argue that without a universal reference point or standard of arbitration, we have no way of detecting and eliminating the violence within our tradition. Rorty argues, however, that liberal culture has an inbuilt safety mechanism to guard against this problem. There is a paradox here, since liberal "culture is an *ethnos* that prides itself on its suspicion of ethnocentrism—on its ability to increase the freedom and openness of encounters, rather than on its possession of truth."[40] He asks us to give up the inhibitions brought about by the need for universal, rational justification and be deliberately ethnocentric since that is both the more honest form of self-understanding as well as the most productive way of achieving desirable change.

Rorty hopes, then, to advance a weaning process in which we gradually let go of metaphysical needs and distractions. Against critics who insist only universalism can provide a basis for reform, he maintains the tradition of liberalism itself provides us with sufficient political orientation and resources. Indeed, the replacement of philosophical with political questions is what provides the space for improvement:

> If one reinterprets objectivity as intersubjectivity, or as solidarity . . . then one will drop the question of how to get in touch with "mind-independent and language-independent reality." One will replace it with questions like "What are the limits of our community? Are our encounters sufficiently free and open? Has what we have recently gained in solidarity cost us our ability to listen to outsiders who are suffering? To outsiders who have new ideas?" These are political questions rather than metaphysical or epistemological questions.[41]

Rorty urges us not to dress up our struggles in extravagant philosophical baggage. Pursuing the truth as a conceptual necessity of reform, he says, has diverted our attention from concrete efforts to prevent unnecessary suffering and cruelty.[42] We have allowed an historically cultivated psychological need to interfere with a more direct, political mode of theory and practice. Reform occurs, in his view, through gradual modifications in, and enlargement of, our imaginations rather than by revolution. We are able to interpret, describe, and evaluate things differently by remaining open to different perspectives and ideas. But these opportunities for more aesthetic forms of appreciation and perception will be missed if we remain preoccupied and distracted by outdated philosophical anxieties. "I see the culture of the liberal democracies as still providing a lot of opportunities for self-criticism and reform, and my critics on the left as fellow citizens taking advantage of these opportunities. They, however, sometimes seem to see themselves as inhabiting a prison-house, one from which they must escape before starting to tear it down."[43]

Rorty moves in the direction of individuality and aesthetics with his mocking of metaphysical needs: "If you give up on the project of escaping from 'human peculiarities and perspectives,' then the important question will be about what sort of human being you want to become."[44] But before going very far in this direction, Rorty is careful to move closer to the first story about the aftereffects of knowledge in modernity. For as we have just seen, even while he is postmodernist, he still seeks to justify a *collective* mode of self-reassurance. The appropriate form of reassurance derives, in his view, not from universal ideas or beliefs but from shared traditions and a sense of belonging. For Rorty, if there is to be a return to individuality as a result of seeing the groundlessness of beliefs, then it must be kept firmly within the private realm and it must not be allowed to infiltrate politics. Concern with oneself is a pursuit of "self-creating ironists" and the "sort of autonomy" they are in search of "is not the sort of thing that could ever be embodied in social institutions."[45] He insists the "vocabulary of self-creation is necessarily private, unshared, unsuited to argument" while the "vocabulary of justice is necessarily public and shared, a medium for argumentative exchange."[46]

According to Rorty, attempts to extend aesthetic practices of individuality into the public and political realms represent a great danger. He insists the philosophical resources needed to guide such processes of self-transformation could only be made available by sacrificing the political freedom and cultural diversity liberalism has been able to precariously establish. For this reason, he says the ambitions of radical democrats to democratize modern societies beyond liberal parameters are both undesirable and unjustifiable. Such efforts are *unjustifiable*, he claims, because there are no ahistorical and universal standards of measurement around which attempts at self-transformation, as a necessary requirement of democratic expansion, could be guided. Thus, any attempt to impose such standards is *undesirable* since it would invite us to regress behind the thresholds of freedom and tolerance achieved by the liberal democratic order. Make sure the "attempt at authenticity and purity," he says, is privatized "in order to prevent yourself from slipping into a political attitude which will lead you to think that there is some social goal more important than avoiding cruelty."[47]

In the same way that liberals had to bracket out theological issues in order to establish a threshold of tolerance centuries ago, Rorty suggests it is the responsibility of liberals today to indicate why secular philosophy's aspirations toward universality, as the basis of radical democratization, should also be dropped. We must rest content with our historical circumstances, in his view, rather than feed the strain of perfectionism evident in the dissatisfaction with the present order. "[E]ven if the typical character types of liberal democracies *are* bland, calculating, petty, and unheroic," he says, "the prevalence of such people may be a reasonable price to pay for political freedom."[48] Rorty advises that while individuals may safely pursue strong philosophical commitments in the private domain, they should remain loyal to the less demanding requirements and practices of a disenchanted, public world. The political, understood as an historical, collective self-understanding, has primacy while philosophical aesthetics should be reduced to merely personal experiments in self-cultivation.

Thus, in order to both advance a tradition of *liberal* reform as well as accommodate self-creating "ironists," Rorty advocates a clear distinction between public and private. One can remain obligated to the public traditions of liberalism, he argues, while pursuing quite contradictory and transcendent aspirations in private. Universalists such as Habermas, even while endorsing the separation of politics from the aesthetics of individuality, have problems with this division between public and private for the reasons discussed above.

But criticism about Rorty's complacency also emerges from other quarters. Like Habermas, these critics think "postmodern bourgeois liberalism" is insufficient to support tolerance, diversity and justice in the contemporary period. But they seek a better radicalism through a public extension of the aesthetic aspirations that Rorty shoves exclusively into the private realm, not via a Habermasian quest for universal foundations. William Connolly, whose work is studied in the second part of this book, believes that "irony is essential to public discourse because public discourse invariably draws upon contestable ontological themes which impinge upon the treatment of people."[49] Rorty, he claims, exudes a false confidence in his attempt to render liberalism post-metaphysical. Rorty thinks by being explicitly ethnocentric about liberalism we get beyond an artificial need and can come to terms with the fact that our beliefs and values are the product of mere socialization. But here Connolly plays the Rorty role against Rorty by emphasizing that this apparently antifoundationalist view of liberalism still draws on deep metaphysical assumptions, assumptions that turn out to have antidemocratic and antiliberal political implications. Connolly asserts, in particular, that Rorty's view that "socialization goes all the way down"

> legitimizes the hyper-organization of the self to meet the needs of a civilization of economic expansion by treating the human material to be organized as pliable and flexible. It subtracts violence from socialization. Since Rorty shares these cultural predilections it is not too surprising he adopts this ontology of selfhood. What is surprising is that he does not seem to recognize it as a metaphysic, typically treating it as the residue which remains once metaphysics has been subtracted from the domain of the self.[50]

In other words, Rorty capitulates to one of the numerous conservative discourses of selfhood by refusing to engage publicly with the question of individuality. Connolly believes that because basic metaphysical, ontological, and theological assumptions are always invoked in politics it is naive to think they can be ignored. It is not possible, in his view, to separate discussions of "life, death and personal identity" from those dealing with "power, justice and solidarity" as Rorty would like to do with his division between private and public.[51] Connolly argues it is ironic indeed that Rorty, the great philosopher of irony, celebrates contingency and yet insists that the questionable standards and practices of liberal democracy be rendered exempt from critique: "Rorty adamantly resists any sustained effort to rethink and remodel the trajectory of the rich, selfish states."[52]

In order to unsettle the complacency of liberalism, Connolly maintains that citizens need to engage in aesthetic work on themselves. If "we" liberals are to be genuinely pluralistic and tolerant, he says, we must be habitually alert to the contingency of our identity and find ways of dealing with this contingency that do not suppress the differences on which identity depends. And these aesthetic issues must be made a theme of public, democratic discussions, not left simply as a private preoccupation of cultural elites. Connolly finds in the work of Nietzsche a major source of inspiration for thinking about how democracy might be extended beyond its liberal manifestations. He believes the continuation of progressive hopes and struggles for a more democratic world require the development of "a politicized left-Nietzscheanism."[53]

One could ask, though, notwithstanding the cogency of Connolly's arguments about the *indispensability* of the metaphysical, whether this call to reconfigure the relations between politics, aesthetics, and individuality can be sustained. From a political perspective, for instance, can we reasonably expect individual citizens to engage in the complex arts of the self? Does this not, as Rorty claims, reinvoke overambitious conceptions of democracy to be found in traditional socialist and radical ideas? And would it not suppress one of the most important dimensions of politics, the concern for the common and the general that is to hold society together? Moreover, from an individual perspective, one may ask what room there is in politics for aesthetic considerations. Have not previous practitioners of arts of the self such as Socrates and Nietzsche found good reasons for ignoring politics in their concern for serious philosophical themes? Are such arts quintessentially private, nonpolitical practices?

Connolly's approach will be considered in detail in chapters five and six in connection with these questions. His ideas are arguably the most sophisticated representation of a broader stream of thinking in contemporary political theory that goes under the rubric of "agonistic democracy." While both liberalism and communitarianism seek to minimize contest and debate, agonistic approaches to democracy emphasize such contest out of the belief that dealing with difference is what politics is all about. Agonists maintain we need to exercise and enhance our ability to live among diverse kinds of people. A restriction of political interaction only to that which can be agreed on is always provisional and ultimately impossible. In the view of agonistic democrats, moreover, such a restriction will actually create more undesirable forms of conflict and injustice in the long term.

Each of the theoretical protagonists in contemporary debates about democracy comes to terms in a particular way with what Honig refers to as "two coexisting and conflicting impulses" in political life:

> the desire to decide crucial undecidabilities for the sake of human goods that thrive most vigorously in stable, predictable settings, and the will to contest established patterns, institutions, and identities for the sake of the remainders engendered by their patternings and for the sake of the democratic possibilities endangered by their petrifactions.[54]

The final chapter aims to combine the insights gathered throughout this book so as to put together a distinctive perspective on how to best address these competing aspects of politics. The argument goes against Connolly's specific conception of the relations between politics, aesthetics, and individuality, even while it draws considerably on his contribution.

The Chapters that Follow

Part I of this book is a defense of the second story about the aftereffects of knowledge in modernity over and against the first. As stated above, Jürgen Habermas is considered here to be the key representative of those persistent efforts to sustain the cognitive-theoretical foundations of modernity. Habermas's work, given its depth and comprehensive range, is a formidable account of why modern ethical and political life requires grounding in a universal form of knowledge. As Thomas McCarthy remarks, Habermas's

> contributions to philosophy and psychology, political science and sociology, the history of ideas and social theory are distinguished not only by their scope but by the unity of perspective that informs them. This unity derives from a vision of mankind, our history and our prospects, that is rooted in the tradition of German thought from Kant to Marx, a vision that draws its power as much from the moral-political intention that animates it as from the systematic form in which it is articulated.[55]

The argument in part one, "Returning to Ourselves," is that Habermas's systematic intention cannot be defended. The claims developed in the three chapters of this part of the book indicate how Habermas seeks theoretical certainty and reassurance by shifting the object of theory from a concern with the individual and subjectivity to social and intersubjective structures. He believes these structures provide the degree of universality and steadfastness suitable for a theory aimed at uncovering a clear foundation for ethics and politics. Chapter 1, "Recovering the Individual in Critical Theory," launches the contestation of this view by providing a critique of his conceptualization of the relationship between theory and practice. Habermas has argued for the replacement of the philosophy of the subject with the paradigm of intersubjectivity as an appropriate framework for critical theory. The chapter questions the efficacy and desirability of such a project. It suggests that critical theory's aim to connect theory with practical intentions must remain unfulfilled in the terms of this intersubjective approach. It examines weaknesses and problems at both the social-theoretical and philosophical levels of his theory construction. It is argued that a renewed emphasis on a philosophy of subjectivity is required to address this disconnection of theory and practice in Habermas's work. A brief consideration of difficulties in Axel Honneth's attempt to renovate the practical dimensions of critical theory indicates that the intersubjective paradigm poses insurmountable dilemmas for any maneuvering remaining inside it.

A concrete illustration of this general proposition about the need to return to a philosophy of subjectivity is put forward in chapter 2, "Individuality Amid Social Progress." The chapter begins by tracing the concern for progress, central to the contemporary agendas of modern societies, back to the fundamental aspirations of the Enlightenment. Around that time, the belief arose that systematic improvements are made possible by the structural features of modern society and culture, improvements that will gradually release humanity from much of the suffering characterizing its historical past. The chapter argues the persistence of a culture of progress, rather than easing suffering, in fact enhances and mobilizes it for the pursuit of superficial forms of gain. Most important, it is claimed Habermas's attempt to develop a broader and more satisfactory conception of progress fails to address this problem. The chapter proposes that an alternative and more fundamental critique of progressive ideas is required. It reflects on these abstract theoretical questions in connection with the example of the "adolescent crisis." Habermas has reflected on the meaning and significance of this crisis and his considerations are contrasted with empirical material about the role ideas of progress currently play in the context of the adolescent years.

In chapter 3, "Dogmatic Retreats and Skeptical Adventures," the nature and implications of the general contrast between two alternative aftereffects of knowledge are elaborated more fully. The chapter focuses on the role of criticism in achieving progress and identifies its "dogmatic" and "skeptical" modes. It reflects on the categorical distinction between nature and culture that is usually thought to be a condition of possibility of criticism. The rationale for the distinction is that, in comparison to natural laws, norms and conventions are merely relative and, therefore, susceptible to criticism and change. The chapter contests this view and argues critical practice is still possible, and even more productive, when nature and culture are seen to be continuous with one another. Significantly, the contention is put forward that not only modern theorists such as Habermas develop a dogmatic mode of criticism on the basis of a distinction between nature and culture. Postmodern thinkers, such as Judith Butler, whose work is also considered in this chapter, arguably adopt a similar approach. An alternative, skeptical critical mode is then specified in connection with Nietzsche and the ancient skeptics. This skeptical method is based on an identity between nature and culture and has affinities with the aesthetic themes evident in contemporary political theory. The ethical and political implications of this skeptical mode of criticism are also considered in this chapter, as a prelude to the more focused treatment of such implications in the second part of the book.

These three chapters, then, develop various components of the argument that an "inward" turn away from a search for cognitive certainty and to a focus on aesthetic forms of self-cultivation is a necessary and more beneficial "after-effect of knowledge." In chapter 3, in particular, this theme is elaborated with respect to the paradoxical requirements of progress. Progress requires, it is contended, not a progressive ideology in which nature and culture are separated from one another. A return to the individual implies, rather, a less "active" view of the self in relation to processes of cultural change. The conditions of possibility of genuine reform depend on returning to work on those hopes and aspirations that have first given such importance to "external" modes of transformation. In the second part of the book, "Democracy, Aesthetics, and Individuality," the grounds for this return to the individual are subjected to more rigorous examination. Here, a few hesitations are expressed about what is otherwise considered to be a positive shift in attention. The central point is that while an inward turn is persuasive, care needs to be adopted in thinking about the possible spaces of application for the theory and practice of self-cultivation, especially in relation to the practice of politics.

Part II focuses on these themes through an examination of debates about the most appropriate strategies for expanding the democratic elements of liberal democracy. Chapter 4, "Habermas's Democratic Proceduralism," begins an examination of the issues involved in a final encounter with Habermas's attempt to separate politics and morality from the aesthetic themes of individuality. Habermas develops a "deliberative" understanding of democracy in order to understand how radical democratic ideals might transform existing liberal institutions. In general, deliberative theorists accept that a radically participatory form of democracy is simply impractical in the context of modern society. They consider the ways in which participation, discussion, and reasoning can take place within liberal institutions and thereby strengthen their deliberative elements without superseding them. The chapter examines Habermas's deliberative response to one of the difficulties facing radical democratization, namely the capacity of the individual to contribute to a properly democratic organization of social and political life. It draws out the way in which he locates the basic foundations of democracy at the level of institutional and cultural forms of *proceduralism* that are designed to act as compensatory devices for personal fallibility and weakness. Habermas thinks procedures make room for political participation by individuals at the same time as they ease the burden of responsibility for democracy on individuals as such. Once again, however, it is argued that this move away from the individual cannot ultimately succeed. Habermas needs to make room for aesthetic considerations in his theory if he is to adequately conceptualize the possibilities for radical democratization.

Chapter 5, "Democracy and Individuality: Kateb and Connolly," considers ideas about democracy in which aesthetic concerns are given a more central role. It reviews what is loosely termed an "existential" appreciation of the role of the individual in democratic expansion. The focus is on the contemporary reception of the writings of Emerson and Nietzsche in the work of George Kateb and William Connolly, respectively. The claim is put forward that these existential approaches, in which democratic skepticism is itself seen to be the impetus behind the formation of individuality, are superior to the deliberative understanding of how liberal democracy can be reformed. In the concluding parts of the chapter, though, a tension between individual self-development and democratic participation is highlighted. The question entertained is whether the task of strengthening the individual tends to undermine rather than enhance the democratic project. While both Connolly and Kateb seek to mobilize the insights of Nietzsche and Emerson in order to provide a more coherent understanding of democracy, they also acknowledge the cogency of the reasons these earlier thinkers had for resisting central features of democratic participation for the sake of the individual.

What can we conclude about this apparent contradiction between the individual and democracy, and between aesthetics and politics more generally? Chapter 6, "Spaces for Individuality" develops a response to this question. It begins with a critique of Connolly's willingness to politicize aesthetic concerns. The argument is that his approach effectively adds to rather than subtracts from the pressures working against the formation of individuality in the contemporary world. The aesthetic requirements of individuality are, that is, in contradiction with the demands of identity politics. The chapter sets out a different understanding of the relationship between individuality and political participation. It indicates how the practice of aesthetic cultivation is best mobilized as a mode of *preparing* individuals for engagement with politics as opposed to being made part of the substance and content of political interaction as such. It also argues that an individuality freed from political pressures and even minimal demands for political participation is still politically significant. The chapter concludes with the idea that individuality, even when not politically engaged, can be understood as a form of citizenship that represents an important bulwark against the contemporary dynamics of injustice.

PART I

Returning to Ourselves

1

Recovering the Individual in Critical Theory

The critical theory of Jürgen Habermas is often criticized for its failure to connect adequately with practice. It suffers from this problem, say the critics, despite Habermas's self-declared aim of linking theory with practical intentions. From within the tradition of critical theory, such an evaluation usually proceeds in one of two different ways. On the one hand, it may question elements of Habermas's philosophy of "discourse ethics."[1] Here, the formal, procedural and abstract features of Habermas's communicative conception of reason are questioned. These features, it is argued, render his theory incapable of providing a practical orientation for individuals or groups. In particular, the separation of the "right" from the "good" is held to pose insurmountable epistemological and ethical problems. On the other hand, the critique may focus on Habermas's social theory, and on the application of systems theory in particular.[2] The objection, in this respect, concerns Habermas's willingness to accept that his own idea of communicative rationality is denied access from large domains of social and political life. It suggests that insofar as theory and practice are still related, their combination offers little or no resistance to the "colonization of the lifeworld."

Axel Honneth's work has followed these lines of critique simultaneously, leading to a substantial reconstruction of Habermas's work from the inside.[3] In brief, first, Honneth replaces Habermas's focus on "validity claims" with an emphasis on "identity claims" as the key structures underlying social interaction.[4] This complements and modifies the weight given to rational discourse in Habermas by incorporating systematically into critical theory the dynamics of social struggle. Second, Honneth's emphasis on struggle dislodges the explanatory importance of systems theory found in Habermas and leads to an insistence that the structures of the lifeworld have primacy as the motors of historical development. This reshaping of the Habermasian version of critical theory strengthens considerably the connection between theory and practice.

This chapter develops, at first, a critique similar to Honneth's. It takes issue with the role functionalism plays in Habermas's social theory. It calls for a stronger connection between the individual and society in the form of a social psychology. In doing so, however, the chapter questions rather than endorses Honneth's attempt to renovate the practical intentions of critical theory. It claims that he inherits too much of the Habermasian framework to solve the basic problems. The argument is that theory and practice can be linked satisfactorily only when the communications-theoretic foundations of critical theory are displaced by a renewed emphasis on a philosophy of subjectivity or, to put it differently, by a recovery of the individual.

The body of the chapter is divided into four sections. The first section establishes a broad context and perspective for the subsequent inquiry into contemporary critical theory. It outlines basic elements of the ancient or classical approach to questions of freedom, morality and politics. From there, the second section moves to an examination of Habermas's reasons for relativizing the practical and individualistic orientations of classical philosophy with a modern, scientific conception of social theory. It considers, in particular, the consequences of his employment of a functionalist method of theory construction. The third section explores an alternative approach to social theory evident within Habermas's corpus and drawn out explicitly by Honneth. It is argued the "causality of fate" is a better framework for a theory of society that remains connected with practical orientations. The fourth section then examines whether this more intimate relationship between theory and practice can be suitably conceptualized within the philosophical horizon of communications theory. It points to problems in both Habermas's and Honneth's diagnosis and critique of modernity that derive from this horizon and claims that a shift to a philosophy of subjectivity is required.

Back to Basics? Pleasure and Pain

In the *Nicomachean Ethics*, Aristotle argues "the whole concern of both morality and political science must be with pleasures and pains."[5] For Aristotle, "pleasure and pain permeate the whole of life" and "since people choose what is pleasant and avoid what is painful," it is important that individuals be taught "to like and dislike the right things."[6] It is important to note that while the feelings of pleasure and pain themselves cannot be denied or overcome, the individual's approach to them can be a subject of instruction and modification.[7] Genuine education teaches individuals to regulate their lives according to appropriate conceptions of pleasure and pain. It results in a virtuous disposition toward oneself and others, an understanding of how to act that is consistent across various situations and circumstances. For Aristotle, a sincere effort to live in this fashion is necessary for the highest form of happiness—contemplation—and, therefore, self-knowledge.[8]

Plato expresses a similar view through a clarification of right fear.[9] Individuals are motivated to live virtuously, he says, when they learn what should be feared. On the one hand, education through fear, properly understood, induces in students an attitude of modesty and moderation in relation to both pleasure and pain. It allows for a certain freedom and autonomy from "these emotions in us, which act like cords or strings and tug us about."[10] An incorrect approach to fear, on the other hand, entails an underlying anxiety about missing out on worldly goods such as money, recognition, and sensual pleasures. It exacerbates the push and pull of pleasure and pain because these forces are tied, through wrong fear, to external circumstances and other people. The individual is left without any form of autonomy because his or her well-being is made dependent on things outside of his control. From this point of view, lack of morality and virtue are the root causes of conformity and unfreedom.

Both Plato and Aristotle believe knowledge of the dynamics of pleasure and pain is essential for the statesman or -woman. Indeed, they think it is important for anyone interested in constructing a peaceful social order. They emphasize, in particular, the far-reaching implications of habits formed in childhood and the consequent need for education in pleasure and pain at this early stage.[11] The rationale is that each individual has a right to grow up in an environment conducive to the full realization of her potential. Self-realization depends on a mind relatively free of the violence and distractions entailed in an unsublimated pursuit of pleasure and avoidance of pain. Order depends on the ethical conduct of the individual; it is destroyed when the voice of reason, effective only when feelings no longer dominate life, is too weak. Aristotle gives the impression, evident in Plato as well, that proper education usually fights a losing battle.

> For it is the nature of the many to be ruled by fear rather than by shame, and to refrain from evil not because of the disgrace but because of the punishments. Living under the sway of their feelings, they pursue their own pleasures and the means of attaining them, and shun the pains that are their opposite; but of that which is fine and truly pleasurable they have not even a conception, since they have never had a taste of it. What discourse could ever reform people like that? To dislodge by argument habits long embedded in the character is a difficult if not impossible task.[12]

Contradictory feelings, which grow stronger without the regulation of education, are not simply opposed to reason. They also enlist reason in their service by invoking "rational" justifications and defenses. Entire worldviews develop on the basis of particular economies of pleasure and pain in which good and evil are contrasted with one another. This process cultivates a limiting form of consciousness in which the individual becomes absorbed in efforts of self-justification, thus distorting systematically the potential for discussion and discourse. The task of political philosophy is to identify and clarify this process and guard against it. It should aim to distinguish between two basic ways of living, the moral and the immoral. The immoral approach, on the one hand, encourages the pursuit of superficial needs such as material comfort, social recognition and self-seeking generally. Its consequence is the disintegration of the individual and society. The moral point of view, on the other hand, encourages individuals to resist peer pressure and worldly rewards, take care of their soul, and build, thereby, the foundations of a peaceful social order.

Plato and Aristotle are not alone in the ancient world in emphasizing such an approach to individual conduct and social order. They express a framework of thinking about ethics that, despite important differences, is shared across the spectrum of classical philosophical traditions.[13] Thus, while the reconsideration of themes such as the role of character and the emotions in morality and politics has often been inspired by an interest in Aristotle, the resources available extend beyond Aristotelianism. A *general* contrast between the ancient and modern theoretical perspectives proves useful in questioning what may often seem to be the incontestable assumptions and conclusions of the latter. This is particularly so with regard to the relationship between theory and practice, since theorists like Plato and Aristotle confront individuals with a clear, practical choice about how to live along with an analysis of the implications of that choice. Habermas believes this kind of direct relationship can no longer be upheld. The remainder of this chapter sets out and questions the various reasons he puts forward for this view. It looks, first, at the category of social-theoretical reasons before examining the more strictly philosophical rationale.

Weakening the Link Between Theory and Practice

Habermas argues the structure of classical political philosophy must be modified substantially under present conditions, even though its moral and practical aspirations should be retained.[14] His reasoning focuses on the historical changes in both the make-up of society and the methods for analyzing them. In terms of social theory, the explanatory power of the social sciences, particularly since the end of the eighteenth century, has displaced the ethical priorities of classical studies. "Political science" has been established, maintains Habermas, on the model of the experimental sciences, a paradigm whose ground was prepared by thinkers such as Machiavelli and Hobbes. This shift has altered the raison d'être of theory away from a focus on individual moral behavior, and how the community should be arranged accordingly, to an emphasis on society as a whole and how its institutional structures can be organized to achieve certain aims and goals. Hobbes, for example, hoped to develop a universal social and political model that would guarantee peace. Likewise, other modern theories with different normative orientations employ scientific methods to justify their arguments. Habermas spells out the potential implications of this shift in approach as follows:

> With a knowledge of the general conditions for a correct order of the state and of society, practical prudent action of human beings toward each other is no longer required, but what is required instead is the correctly calculated generation of rules, relationships, and institutions. . . . The engineers of the correct order can disregard the categories of ethical social intercourse and confine themselves to the construction of conditions under which human beings, just like objects within nature, will necessarily behave in a calculable manner.[15]

Habermas wishes to avoid this technocratic extreme through a combination of the modern and classical perspectives. On the one hand, he insists on incorporating the scientific method into political and social theory because only such a method can be adequate to the complexity of modern society. It is desirable, first, for the Hobbesian rationale: a degree of social engineering is essential to achieve some moral aspirations. Second, and more generally, a scientific theory of social evolution can ascertain the appropriate level of complexity required by a given stage of development and thereby justify the restriction of demands for human freedom and control over social processes.[16] On the other hand, Habermas is aware that the conditions of realization of technological potentials are outside the scope of science itself. The benevolent application of mechanical knowledge is dependent on moral and practical capacities: "the scientific control of natural and social processes . . . does not release men from action. Just as before, conflicts must be decided, interests realized, interpretations found—through both action and transaction structured by ordinary language."[17] Similarly, identification of an "appropriate" level of complexity cannot be reduced completely to scientific investigation. The underlying intentions of the classical approach, for these reasons, remain indispensable.

The aim of reconciling theory and practice in this way has always underlain Habermas's work. At one point, he expresses this intention in terms of the following questions:

> how can the promise of practical politics—namely, of providing practical orientation about what is right and just in a given situation—be redeemed without relinquishing, on the one hand, the rigor of scientific

> knowledge, which modern social philosophy demands in contrast to the practical philosophy of classicism? And on the other, how can the promise of social philosophy, to furnish an analysis of the interrelationships of social life, be redeemed without relinquishing the practical orientation of classical politics?[18]

Habermas fails, in my view, to respond to these questions satisfactorily. The remainder of this section develops the first stage of this argument in terms of a critique of his social theory.

Habermas has most favored a "functionalist" form of inquiry in his construction of social theory. This methodology is suited, as stated above, to addressing the question of social order. The key concepts are "system" and "lifeworld" that identify two frameworks of action coordination. They explain the conditions of societal integration by pointing out the "unconscious" dimensions of stability. On the one hand, there are intersubjective structures of the lifeworld, divided into the realms of "culture," "society" and "personality." Here, action is coordinated on the basis of an interlocking of intentions, a process supported by a "sprawling, deeply set, and unshakeable rock of background assumptions, loyalties, and skills."[19] On the other hand, the media of money and power structure the systemic domains of economy and state, neutralize lifeworld contexts and circumscribe action in a methodical way. In the case of the lifeworld, "participants remain intuitively aware of orders established by social integration even if this takes the form of a prereflexive, by no means readily available or recallable background knowledge." But in the case of systems, order is "as a rule counterintuitive in nature."[20] Individual *actions* of various types occur within the environments of both system and lifeworld but are subject to the constraints of an overarching framework. While ordinary language provides an infrastructure of support that allows individuals to cooperate freely, systemic media constrain and condition thought and action within narrow opportunities for choice.

This functionalist mode of analysis is, as noted earlier, a means via which a conception of practical conduct can be complemented with a scientific understanding of society. More important, it is essential, in Habermas's view, so as to avoid the heavy reliance on action theory characteristic of the critical theory tradition.[21] It represents a way of transcending the problems invoked by a social theory relying on the philosophy of the subject. One manifestation of these problems, for Habermas, occurs in Marx's formulation of socialist and radical democratic ideals. Marx had conceived social evolution in terms of the movement of an ethical totality or macrolevel subject that divides itself against itself (capitalism) only to then reabsorb the fragmented elements within a higher-level synthesis (socialism). In Habermas's view, this conception of diremption followed by dialectical integration cannot and should not be sustained: "Systems theory and action theory can be viewed as the *disjecta membra* of th[e]

Hegelian-Marxist heritage."[22] He insists a conception of modern history in terms of system and lifeworld makes clear there is an "intrinsic evolutionary value" to the development of "media-steered subsystems." Marx's approach, however, "excludes from the start the question of whether" these developments "represent a higher and evolutionarily advantageous level of integration by comparison to traditional societies."[23] Habermas wishes to theoretically guard against desires for large-scale revolutionary change. The unintended consequences of such interference are unforeseeable and should be approached with great caution. He believes this "must make the *juste milieu* appear more and more worth preserving, even in the eyes of those who have not given up the expectation of a long-term revolutionary transformation."[24] The system-social integration dichotomy makes this clear and allows Habermas to recommend the more modest goal of "erect[ing] a democratic dam against the colonializing *encroachment* of system imperatives on areas of the lifeworld."[25]

A number of criticisms of this application of systems theory have already been developed in the literature. These criticisms generally focus on Habermas's suggestion of an ontological dichotomy between system and lifeworld.[26] He had, for example, described systems as a "norm-free sociality," implying the administrative-bureaucratic and economic spheres are immune to democratic and communicative reform. To a certain degree, this problem has been addressed by Habermas's subsequent clarifications, clarifications used in the above characterization of his functionalist approach: the concept of system refers not to action types but to the *framework* of action and interaction.[27] The ideas developed in *Between Facts and Norms* make it more explicit that systemic realms are not closed completely to communicative intervention, either from without or within. Habermas's idea that internal to law is a discursive democratic structure, in particular, indicates how democratic impulses can penetrate systemically integrated domains.

To a considerable extent, though, Habermas only *appears* to elude this general criticism by exploiting inconsistencies in his approach that allow him to waver on the exact significance of systems theory. Barbara Herrnstein Smith has analyzed closely such mechanisms of self-defence in contemporary intellectual controversies, as well as in particular aspects of Habermas's moral theory.[28] She points out the way theorists, in defending their position, often simultaneously recognize a substantial problem at the same time as refusing to follow through its implications. The superficial consequence of such a strategy is that one's position is strengthened. In the case of Habermas's defence of discourse ethics, she notes how he "repeatedly acknowledges but does not *acknowledge* acknowledging" the cogency of skeptical objections.[29] McCarthy makes a similar observation in regard to Habermas's negotiations with systems theory: "Habermas grants the premises [of significant criticisms of systems theory] but resists the conclusion."[30] Even while Habermas often admits the symbolic nature of social life grates heavily against the tools of systems theory, his *actual* analyses and diagnoses presume the cogency of a systems-theoretical perspective. He tends, in particular, to work with a dichotomy of system and lifeworld, to characterize a particular domain as *either* socially *or* systemically integrated. He assumes, in McCarthy's words, if "the objective sense of an action i[s] not intuitively present to the actor" it must be "a matter of latent functionality," that is, a matter for conceptualization in terms of systems theory.[31]

There is no compelling reason to think, however, that the unconscious elements of social life need to be explained by systems theory. Habermas's dichotomous method excludes a possibility that may suit most circumstances most of the time: namely, social life is integrated neither by complete mutual understanding nor systemic interconnection but by a mixture of understandings, misunderstandings, unconscious pressures and strategic force. This general point has been made from the other side as it were, with regard to Habermas's tendency to treat the lifeworld as a rationalized sphere without ideology or pathology.[32] As Bohman argues, it would be a significant mistake to think the potential for ideology has disappeared from modern society, as Habermas makes out, and only systemic colonization of an innocent lifeworld is the central problem.[33] The dichotomy between system and lifeworld examines merely an external relationship and prevents an understanding of how the domains are interconnected and interrelated. Systems theory does not at all conceptualize adequately the inner constitution and dynamics of systems but only the external interaction of the system with its environment.[34] Yet, the inner dynamics of systems may well be made up of their so-called external environment. Moreover, from a social democratic point of view, there are good reasons for focusing on the contradictions of these inner dynamics.

Justifiably, Habermas has wished to weaken the strong link between theory and practice to be found in some areas of the Marxist tradition. He intends to reconstruct and clarify the conditions of possibility for what, in the end, can only be decided by participants themselves. Habermas's employment of systems theory, nevertheless, contradicts this aim. As Benhabib remarks, Habermas's theory of history is less a reconstructive hypothesis open to empirical verification than a philosophical narrative that tends to "speak in the name of a fictional collective 'we' from whose standpoint the story of history is told."[35] In a mirror image of Marx, Habermas "excludes from the start" the question of whether systemic structures are *not* an evolutionary advance that should remain open to criticism and radical modification. In other words, the problems Habermas had hoped to dissolve by abandoning the philosophy of the subject reappear.

If systems theory is neither theoretically nor politically compelling, therefore, it may be appropriate to adopt an alternative approach. In particular, if theory is to remain connected with practice, I would argue it is important that social theory not be separated from the motivations for thought and action of individuals themselves. Habermas had suggested this at an earlier point in his theoretical development:

> A sociology that accepts meaning as a basic concept cannot abstract the social system from structures of personality; it is always also social psychology. The system of institutions must be grasped in terms of the imposed repression of needs and of the scope for possible individualization, just as personality structures must be grasped in determinations of the institutional framework and of role qualifications.[36]

The next section of the chapter examines an alternative strand of thought in Habermas's work which provides a social-psychological alternative to systems theory. It leads from his reflections on the idea of the "causality of fate."

RECONNECTING THEORY WITH PRACTICE: THE "CAUSALITY OF FATE"

Habermas's concept of the "causality of fate" is based on his central philosophical claim about social practice, that the formation of individual identity comes about through "taking the attitude of the other."[37] He claims this mechanism enables the individual to see his own behavior from the perspective of others. It is only with this, says Habermas, that the individual comes into view to himself. Self-consciousness arises in a context of interaction, in the form of letting go of an entirely egoistical perspective. This move from a centered to a decentered frame of reference is an expanded capacity for perception. According to Habermas, an important implication follows when we understand this dependency of the individual on a context of interaction with others. The identity of human beings can be stable only when individuals maintain a specific form of interaction, one in which *reciprocity* is secured. This is so because individuals cannot "have" their identity as a possession; identity or individuality contains an "intersubjective core."[38] Identity is an attribute that can be formed and sustained when each person takes into account the needs and interests of all others. Identity is necessarily injured and damaged *for both parties* in relationships of exploitation. When an individual does not recognize others, they cannot recognize themselves *as an individual.* If they treat others as objects, they take away a point of view from which they themselves could come into view as a subject rather than as an object to be manipulated.

For Habermas, the features of language use mean that individuals, to form an inward sense of identity, must enter on the unstable terrain of interpersonal relations. It is through this risky process of relating to others, and through this process alone, that one can gain a personality oneself. In doing so, the subject exposes itself to the reliability and sense of concern of its interaction partners. Habermas argues nonreciprocal or noncommunicative forms of action are parasitic on the human way of life. The fundamental intuitions of moral theory are, from this point of view, anthropologically rooted. They represent "a safety device compensating for a vulnerability built into the sociocultural form of life."[39] Morality protects the "almost constitutional insecurity and chronic fragility of personal identity—an insecurity that is antecedent to cruder threats to the integrity of life and limb."[40]

Habermas claims that when the fragile framework of intersubjectivity is disrupted in some way, individuals immediately feel the repercussions. Communicative structures represent a net within which all humans are linked together. The effects of isolated disturbances spread out radially in all directions along connecting pathways.[41] For Habermas, these disturbances explain, at the level of individual psychology, a great deal of human suffering: damaged communicative fabrics are inhabited by unstable individuals. He describes the overarching conceptual framework in which such disruptions can be understood in terms of Hegel's idea of the "causality of fate" or "dialectic of the moral life."[42] Hegel refers to the "criminal" who "annuls the complementarity of unconstrained communication and the reciprocal gratification of needs by putting himself as an individual in place of the totality." This sets off a fateful struggle "ruled by the power of the suppressed life."[43] The struggle ends only when the parties to it restore reciprocal relations and, thereby, their mutually dependent identities.

This general idea can be elaborated at two different levels.[44] Habermas has preferred to apply it mainly at an intellectual level in arguments with poststructuralists and moral skeptics. It leads, when linked with the concept of "validity claims," to the notion of "performative contradiction." Habermas claims theorists such as Foucault or Derrida commit this contradiction by putting forward claims to validity that are in conflict with the presuppositions logically entailed in making those claims. They set off, in his view, a fateful process of logic that rebounds on them in argumentative practice. Habermas, in defending a universalistic rationality and cognitivist concept of morality, purports merely to register the intellectual dynamics of this causality of fate. The notion of validity claims is derived from the system of "performative verbs" that form part of a series of basic distinctions fundamental to any speech situation. The structure of speech situations is also composed of an equally important element, the system of "personal pronouns." The personal pronouns refer not to claims to validity, to claims about statements, but to the identity claims described earlier, the claims subjects make to be recognized as subjects. A discourse in which claims to validity are thematized and contested presupposes the redemption of identity claims. For this reason, Habermas stresses that "identity claims aiming at intersubjective recognition must not be confused with the validity claims that the actor raises with his speech acts. For the 'no' with which the addressee rejects a speech-act offer concerns the validity of a particular utterance, not the identity of the speaker."[45]

The causality of fate is also applicable at the level of identity, as has already been implied. Axel Honneth has mobilized this insight in elaborating his theory of the "struggle for recognition." This theory charts an historical movement toward emancipation propelled onward by the denial of subjects' need for recognition. The struggle aims to reestablish relations of reciprocity at a number of levels. Habermas's focus on validity claims in his theory of communicative action means the construction of social theory is left over to a conceptualization in terms of systems. Honneth, on the other hand, in bringing claims to identity to the foreground, displaces the need and importance of systems theory and privileges the causality of fate as the framework for understanding the dynamics of modernity. With this, the more substantive elements of Habermas's theory are highlighted and a link with practical orientations is regained. Honneth's intervention is, therefore, significant although it may also be viewed as "only an extension and a further development of what is already implicit in Habermas's theory."[46] Further discussion of Honneth's approach takes place at the end of the chapter. For now, I would like to elaborate the possible implications of the causality of fate for Habermas's employment of systems theory.

Habermas notes it is the criminal's "act of tearing loose from an intersubjectively shared lifeworld [which] first *generates* a subject-object relationship."[47] The significance of the introduction of subject-object relationships is that an unconscious element emerges in the interaction system. Communication is consensual, free and autonomous, for Habermas, only when the motives and intentions of individuals can be articulated and expressed consciously in the form of norms. Subject-object relations, which have spread throughout modern society via the economic, political, and cultural scarring of communicative interaction, exclude normative regulation. Significantly, this structuring of relationships creates a distorted understanding of freedom. Habermas argues that when we are clear about the communicative construction of the self, it is obvious that freedom and independence cannot be arrived at "by detaching [one]self from particular life contexts," by "step[ing] outside of society altogether and settl[ing] down in a space of abstract isolation and freedom."[48] This delusion becomes compelling, however, insofar as individuals are alienated from a life whose rules and regulations are the outcome of a cooperative discussion. They get the impression freedom lies in the direction of expanding strategic power over others. This understanding and the action flowing from it merely reinforces the initial repression of the conditions of possibility of identity. The problem is that what is required to restore conscious regulation and identity now appears to be a sacrifice of one's own interests. For Habermas, if this can be overcome, one learns, again, how to see oneself through the eyes of the other, thereby regaining an intersubjective capacity for thought and action. It is the deep-seated prejudice ingrained within modern consciousness by subject-object relationships that systematically obstructs this different path of development.

An understanding of how the causality of fate leads to the development of a specific syndrome of mentalities, attitudes and intentions may be a way of conceptualizing "systems" that does not presume they are evolutionary superior steering mechanisms. It could indicate how systemic structures are not mutually exclusive to forms of social integration but are, instead, bound up with the personality traits of individuals. From this point of view, "systemic structures" represent an underdeveloped moral consciousness rather than a necessary form of historical progress. In addition, individuals reappear in the critical theory of society as authors of their own fate. They choose, consciously or unconsciously, to follow one of two basic conceptions of freedom. Critical theory, in clarifying those choices, provides both an explanation of social reproduction and a starting point for various political and pedagogical attempts to make those choices a topic of reconsideration.

Such a social psychological point of view may seem to be subject to the same criticism that Habermas directs at Marx, that it reduces to moral terms what can only be understood as an evolutionary process. As argued above, though, Habermas tends to prejudge this *empirical* question from the other side. Moreover, the social psychological perspective can be defended as both more impartial than, and more consistent with, Habermas's own reconstructive approach. Interpreting systems as forms of restricted communication allows, first, for objectivity because it in no way prevents recognition that these restrictions contribute to efficiency, productivity, and free time from the demands of labor; and, second, for consistency with the ideals of communicative rationality because it reopens explicitly a syndrome of mentalities and motivations to the possibility of discursive transformation.

Communicative Versus Subject-Centered Reason

A recovery of the individual in Habermas's social theory strengthens critical theory's practical orientation. It may not be enough to relink theory and practice satisfactorily, though, since Habermas has developed other, philosophical methods of avoiding the individual. On the philosophical plane of analysis, he insists that explanations of the origins of self-consciousness and of the nature of relationships between individuals are marred by indissoluble problems when elaborated from within the philosophy of the subject. In his view, the communications-theoretic explication, summarized very briefly above, renders these problems "objectless" or "pointless."[49] Habermas declares the "paradigm of the philosophy of consciousness is exhausted" and "with the transition to the paradigm of mutual understanding" these "symptoms of exhaustion should dissolve."[50] The essential point, for him, is that the dilemmas thrown up by a philosophy insisting on the primacy of subjectivity rather than intersubjectivity can be set aside once we realize the subject does not exist in itself but emerges only in a context of interaction.

This chicken-and-the-egg debate may be interminable.[51] I would like to bypass a direct examination of the complex issues involved and mention just one important point that emerges from elements of the critical commentary. This point is that while Habermas's move to a paradigm of intersubjectivity may well be significant and even persuasive in many respects, it does not achieve all that he claims for it. It does not, in particular, "dissolve" the problems of the philosophy of consciousness but, in Dews's formulation, merely "sidelines" them by emphasizing the significance of a different set of issues and problems.[52] The original problems and issues persist, in other words, only they are now considered much less relevant than before.[53] These problems and issues involve the subject's relation to itself, the "dimension of private subjective interiority" left "completely unplumbed" by Habermas's focus on intersubjectivity.[54] In this final section of the chapter, I would like to offer a reappraisal of the significance of these problems and issues. Rather than examine the more strictly explanatory questions, however, I will focus on the ethical and political dimensions of the tensions between subjectivity and intersubjectivity.

From my reading, it seems a general fear of the political implications of a concrete, ethical mode of philosophy informs Habermas's theory. Habermas thinks, first, a philosophy claiming universal applicability and intending to provide existential orientation is dangerous and totalitarian. Authoritative discussion of the good life is supposed to violate the pluralistic conditions of modern societies. In this connection, an important rationale of the theory of communicative action is to overcome the dependence of earlier critical theory on the particular and exclusionary norms of bourgeois society. Habermas seeks an anchor in structures of everyday practice whose origins lie "back beyond the threshold of modern societies" rather than in the concrete ideals "specific to a single epoch."[55] This is designed to provide foundations that transcend limitations of time and place and are not prejudiced in favor of historically contingent norms.

Habermas argues, second, this anchor must not be individualistic in character. The emphasis on the "intersubjective core" of identity is meant to establish that the conditions for effective discussion rest in the structures of a linguistic framework external to the consciousness of individuals. This supports, in turn, an evolutionary view of history in which modern culture and political institutions are seen to have developed in order to secure the principle of discussion above that of violence as a means of resolving social problems. The discourse theory of democracy and law, for example, indicates how modern institutions "play the role of 'congealed' or 'sedimented' virtue" thus making "the *actual practice* of . . . virtues, such as truthfulness, wisdom, reason, justice and all kinds of exceptional moral qualities, to some extent dispensable—on the part of both the rulers and the ruled."[56]

Habermasian critical theory finds its foundations not in individuals but in much larger structures that function to "steer" individual behavior along desirable pathways. These considerations help explain why the basic idea of communicative action, and the concept of the lifeworld connected to it, is imbued with a functionalist hue. Yet Habermas's attempt to avoid the individual at all costs does not achieve his aims. First, there is the mistaken suggestion that identifying norms at an abstract, intersubjective level avoids the problem of "telling people what to do" in a liberal culture. In Habermas's thinking, this abstraction makes possible a strictly reconstructive approach: one that clarifies only what is always already the case and thereby does not preempt autonomy and freedom with directives about what should be done. The reconstructive ideal, nonetheless, is not tied necessarily to this *kind* of abstraction. The concreteness of classical philosophy, for example, can also be interpreted reconstructively. Plato and Aristotle present clear accounts of the moral and the immoral ways of life in such a way that the individual is stimulated to reflect on his or her current condition. Habermas's reservations are misplaced insofar as he thinks this perspective has an indissoluble connection with a particular way of life. A philosophy which stresses "the importance of the good does not need the community dimension."[57] A theory interested in the good life can be based, rather, in a conception of character able to claim universality without compromising pluralism because it refers to abstract dispositions not tied up with specific communitarian claims. Aristotle emphasizes both the abstractness and practical focus of philosophy when he insists the aim is ultimately practical rather than theoretical. Even though a *theory* responds to the question, "How should I live?" it still compels "the agents . . . at every step to think out for themselves what the circumstances demand."[58]

Second, significant dangers are created by the abstractive and functionalizing tendencies within Habermas's work. These tendencies neither leave things open to the participants, nor do they identify a surer foundation for democratic order. Even though Habermas's approach is motivated by respect for individual autonomy, it ends up putting this autonomy at risk because of what it prioritizes and leaves out. The emphasis on basic moral rights and freedoms, in particular, represents a privileging of protection against outward "personal injury" over inward "spiritual desperation."[59] This minimal outlook is best elaborated in a philosophy of communication because the latter deemphasizes the world of inner experience. But without a firmer direction or guidance for interaction, individuals are left only to the dominant tendencies of the age as frameworks for interpreting themselves and the world. *Critical* theory, to this extent, fails to provide effective opposition to the worldviews that arise out of the dynamics of the causality of fate. Habermas's approach becomes vulnerable to a criticism he had referred to in relation to systems theory and its inbuilt arguments against revolutionary change. In "anxiously striving to avoid at all costs catastrophes that are provoked," his strictures against a more substantial mode of philosophizing "not only fail to protect us from catastrophe that makes its way in a quasi-natural fashion—fascistic catastrophe—but deliver us up to it."[60]

In general, then, the movement away from the individual found in Habermas's theory of communicative action significantly enfeebles the relation between theory and practice. It also fails to ease the fears motivating it. Habermas insists, though, that a connection between theory and practice is essential to the identity of critical theory. The remainder of this section of the chapter examines a further set of problems that derive from these weaker practical implications. To make clear these problems derive from the communications-theoretic paradigm as such, an inverse set of dilemmas is also considered in connection with Axel Honneth's version of critical theory. To set up this interpretation, I will begin with a few observations made by Nancy Fraser about contemporary struggles against injustice.[61] Fraser discusses, among other things, the tensions between the short- and long-term dimensions of a strategy of emancipation. The easiest way to motivate disaffected groups for political action, she notes, is to affirm their existing identities against suffered injustice. Drawing attention to an economic class, a sexual group or a racial minority identifies the addressees such a politics is trying to agitate. The emotional and affective potential attached to existing experiences of injustice offers an energy basis for action. A more radical and "truthful" approach, however, cannot make such concessions. The lure of a short-term appeal must be bypassed for the sake of a more fundamental and demanding questioning of the nature of identities. What Fraser describes as a "deconstructive and socialist" politics is "far removed from the immediate interests and identities" of most of those concerned. If this strategy is to be "psychologically and politically feasible," people will need to be "weaned from their attachment to current cultural constructions of their interests and identities."[62] Each of these strategies has, then, a particular economy of advantages and disadvantages.

The tension between the short- and long-term aspects of struggle has been a perennial issue in progressive politics. It is argued here that rather than resolving this problem, the communications paradigm of critical theory provides for a link between theory and practice that tends toward one or the other pole but not one that enables a satisfactory consideration of both. To begin with Habermas, we may consider his version of deliberative politics and democracy as an exemplification of his theory's attraction to the long-term aspect of change. Deliberation, in Habermas's sense, is very demanding. Both the liberal pursuit of self-interest and the republican commitment to the norms and values of one's community of belonging need to be tempered substantially so as to make room for reflection on broader interests. Living in this way is moral, it aspires to universality, but it is also exacting. A deliberative approach requires considerable time and energy, a willingness and ability to question one's needs and interests and be empathetic towards those of others. Individuals need to be independent enough to resist the lures held out to them by both the liberal and republican traditions. My objection is not to the strong normative aspirations of this perspective, but to the weak model of philosophy that supports it.

Habermas, in his request for deliberation, fails to meet individuals halfway by being meager in philosophical substance. As established earlier, the importance of identity claims means that engaging constructively in a demanding discourse implies individuals will have resolved many questions about their life as a whole. These broad, existential questions are, nevertheless, outside the scope of philosophy for Habermas. He has sought, instead, to develop a theory of how discursive structures develop and function so as to create the conditions of possibility of deliberation. In place of addressing the individual prerequisites of discourse, he has focused only on functional and linguistic factors. Such theoretical efforts ignore the evident truth, though, that "people of good character can 'live together well' without complicated procedures or far-fetched assumptions."[63] This truth implies the need for a mode of philosophizing that addresses questions of morality and ethics in a substantial way. To be sure, acknowledging individual character as an important ground of politics does not provide us with foundations of the kind that Habermas hopes for. Character is variable in a way that structures of linguistic interaction are not. The object of theory need not, however, be the identification of foundations in this sense. Philosophy, rather, might better serve morality and ethics by becoming more sensitive and responsive to the ambiguities and contingencies of their practice.

This rationalistic one-sidedness in Habermas's approach is remedied in Axel Honneth's restructuring of critical theory. Honneth seeks to provide more substance by outlining a notion of *ethical life* that is nevertheless universalist, one which can be "extracted from the plurality of all particular forms of life."[64] In focusing on claims to identity, he insists social conflicts are hardly ever purely instrumental in character but relate to the underlying relations of recognition on which the identities of the participants depend. Honneth argues "successful ego-development presupposes a certain sequence of forms of reciprocal recognition."[65] The role of critical theory is to make clear how the denial of identity claims obstructs this developmental process and can lead subjects to "see themselves obliged to engage in a 'struggle for recognition.'" He identifies three forms of recognition (love, respect, and solidarity) that constitute the "structural elements of ethical life." In turn, he specifies three corresponding forms of disrespect that help to explain "the motivational impetus for social resistance and conflict."[66] He maintains "the experience of disrespect is always accompanied by affective sensations that are, in principle, capable of revealing to individuals the fact that certain forms of recognition are being withheld from them."[67]

Honneth's emphasis on the identity claims of individuals, in comparison to Habermas's focus on validity claims, means theory can link up with practice by responding to felt needs. To return to the discussion of Fraser, though, Honneth's outlook, while being more substantial, appears to capitulate to a short-term but unfruitful strategy of emancipation. It articulates and mobilizes an energy basis for action and struggle but, in doing so, may well reinforce rather than question the relevant identities. Once again, I would argue the communications-theoretic paradigm produces these problems. The emphasis on communication and recognition signifies the focus of theory is on the conditions of identity outside the individual. Honneth insists it is only "with the help of their interaction partners" that human subjects can acquire freedom and happiness, through more symmetrical structures of recognition.[68] Of course, support from others, especially when a person is very young, is crucial to the formation of identity, as Honneth emphasizes with the category of "love." Throughout life, a variety of cultural, social, economic and interpersonal sources of assistance are similarly significant. Nonetheless, inward conditions of thought and action may be equally, if not more important in many ways. For each person, a level of freedom and detachment *from* needs for recognition is indispensable. As Dieter Henrich remarks in connection with Habermas, "anyone who is able to turn a discussion towards measure and truth must have achieved a certain level of insight concerning himself."[69] Struggles for recognition will be unable to achieve long-term goals if they neglect such "inner" concerns. Establishing a just and good society requires reflection and conduct that is, paradoxically, both free from and inspired by dissatisfaction with the present order of things.[70]

In conclusion, there is a widespread perception that modern societies are suffering from a high level of alienation and exploitation. Do struggles for recognition grounded in emotional deprivations represent a desirable response to this predicament? Or, given the interpenetration of the structures of society with the personality characteristics of individuals, is the legitimation of such struggles potentially part of the problem? Clearly, the modern world is filled with injustices that need to be addressed through struggle and agitation. Such methods may be fruitful, however, only if they are mobilized by subjects who have already attained a certain level of independence within themselves. The issues involved in achieving such independence cannot be addressed adequately without a philosophy of subjectivity. Contemporary critical theory will therefore remain deficient unless it makes room for such a philosophy and recovers a conception of individuality. The following two chapters seek to elaborate, in different ways, on how the required notion of individuality might be understood.

2

Individuality Amid Social Progress

Contemporary critical theory needs to rehabilitate a concern for individuality. One way of doing this was indicated in the previous chapter: displacing the overly functionalist orientation deriving from Habermas's focus on linguistic and systemic structures with a social psychology of pleasure and pain. This chapter pursues this suggestion further through an examination, at both the theoretical and empirical levels, of the links between politics, suffering, progress, and individuality. The context of the discussion is the widening gap in modern societies between citizens' expectations and their actual conditions of existence. There is a rising level of suffering in Western countries which has significant implications when governments fail repeatedly to deliver on their rhetoric of amelioration. For confidence in the capacities of politics to solve social and economic problems is in a state of decline, even while demands for political solutions persist. One of the most obvious consequences of these developments is the relative success at the polls of electoral candidates from outside the mainstream. There may, however, be much broader and deeper implications other than these surface cracks in the stability of political systems. A general belief in progress, as espoused by major political parties along with other important institutions, appears to be dissolving. This chapter examines the diffuse cultural mood in which the contemporary politics of suffering takes place in order to rethink the validity of the idea of progress in relation to the requirements of individuality. It reflects on the issues involved in connection with the concrete example of the "adolescent crisis" and the role conceptions of progress play within it.

The chapter begins with a brief review of the rise and fall of Enlightenment hopes that human suffering would be reduced substantially or even brought to an end through historical progress. It then outlines, in the second section, Habermas's concern with this loss of faith and his attempt to renew it. Habermas sustains the tradition of critical theory by seeking to make practical the idea that modern forms of rationality and social organization are fundamentally progressive. He does so by identifying groups that are motivated, because of their social conditions, to act as agencies of change and realize extant potentials for improvement. The third section of the chapter examines Habermas's specific thesis that the "adolescent crisis" could be such a trigger for further development in moral freedom and independence. It is argued, using Australian research into the mental health and well-being of young people today, that the evidence contradicts this thesis. Analysis of the trajectory of the adolescent crisis may even provide good reasons for doubting the progressive philosophy of history as a general framework of critical interpretation. The final section elaborates on these reasons and suggests that the belief in progress needs to be rethought significantly. The claim is that attempts to reconstruct a culture of progress, under present conditions, will feed into rather than prevent a destructive politics of suffering and intensify the pursuit of only superficial forms of gain. The development of individuality, by contrast, requires detachment from the belief in progress in order to cultivate an aesthetic mode of perception and understanding.

The Politics of Suffering

Suffering is a primordial and ubiquitous feature of human life. People suffer from a multitude of problems and difficulties, some of which are obvious and clearly observable while others are more subtle and invisible. Moreover, a considerable proportion of human activity is motivated, in one way or another, by an interest in reducing suffering. In contemporary circumstances, political struggles at a number of different levels continue to proliferate in an attempt to diminish or eliminate unnecessary pain and hardship. A convenient framework for understanding these struggles identifies two basic categories of endeavor.[1] One category involves the suffering caused by "distributive injustice," while the other refers to forms of "cultural injustice." In the first category, the relevant discourses of struggle revolve around terms such as "interest" and "exploitation" and aim at equalizing economic opportunities. In the second, the concern is with issues like "identity" and "difference," and a "politics of recognition" seeking to alter the self-understanding of groups that have been defined in negative ways by a dominant culture. While economic forms of deprivation are usually measurable and visible, cultural modes of suffering are less explicit. In this second case, "people suffer from injuries imposed by institutionalized identities, principles, and cultural understandings."[2]

Beyond this apparently unnecessary suffering, there also seems to be a deeper level of distress that may be an inbuilt feature of the human condition.

Suffering, in this existential sense, is pervasive and always bubbling along apart from the added problems imposed by a particular political system or cultural framework. Habermas refers to it in terms of the "basic risks of existence," such as guilt, sickness, and death.[3] The ancient Greek philosophers shared the view that transcending this form of suffering and reaching an enduring condition of happiness was possible only after considerable effort.[4] Without this effort, from Schopenhauer's pessimistic perspective, life consists merely in warding off boredom by a "constant wishing and never being satisfied," of striving and struggling after goals whose value vanishes when we reach them.[5]

Suffering is made more complex because its various levels and dimensions are connected and intertwined. Toward the end of this chapter, there is a further discussion of the relationships between these different aspects. In the meantime, I would like to reflect on the responses that are made to suffering and the implications of these responses. For suffering imposes demands—to be expressed, eased, ended, even continued or revenged. And these reactions to suffering enter into an elaborate world of relations between individuals and groups. The dynamics of suffering are, therefore, an important consideration for any attempt to understand human life. More specifically, they are essential for comprehending politics and culture because these dynamics not only exist in a primary form, but are politically and culturally *organized*.

The philosophy of the Enlightenment can be understood as a particular kind of organized response to suffering. This response was conditioned by the rise of hopes that suffering could be put to an end through historical progress. Thinkers like Condorcet "had the extravagant expectation that the arts and the sciences would promote not only the control of natural forces, but would also further understanding of the world and of the self, would promote moral progress, the justice of institutions, and even the happiness of human beings."[6] From this point of view, the trajectory of Western society and culture expresses a universal and progressive meaning. The expanding power of natural science, with its capacity to control and perhaps eliminate many forms of anguish, was crucial in the emergence of these hopes. It was even thought that further application of scientific methods would dissolve the eternal, dogmatic controversies in philosophy and religion. Karl Löwith has shown how this modern historical consciousness became even more compelling with, first, the practical success of the political and industrial revolutions and, second, the construction of a metaphysical conception of history out of ideas in the Judaeo-Christian tradition.[7] This modern view, he emphasizes, contrasts sharply with earlier conceptions. Previously, history was generally seen as a succession of events that continually threatened human efforts to construct a stable social and political order. Now, it was thought possible that history could be managed and made actively rather than accepted passively as a tragic fate. In comparison to the classical conception of history as a meaningless and endless process of circular change, the modern understanding views history as the very dimension within which human reason is brought to awareness and happiness realized. History is no longer understood as a source of threat, as an unstable sequence of happenings, but as something manageable and the terrain on which certainty and security can be established. Hegel, in particular, elaborated the idea that historical events embody a transcendent meaning that progressively (though dialectically) manifests itself through time.[8]

Belief in this progressive view of history has eroded during the course of modernity, as human suffering has persisted and even intensified in many respects. The confidence of the Enlightenment has given way to a widespread mood of despair and even horror at what the historical process has actually delivered. Habermas offered this summary of such a nihilistic outlook toward the end of the last century:

> Today it seems as though utopian energies have been used up, as if they have retreated from historical thought. . . . The future is negatively cathected; we see outlined on the threshold of the twenty-first century the horrifying panorama of a worldwide threat to universal life interests: the spiral of the arms race, the uncontrolled spread of nuclear weapons, the structural impoverishment of developing countries, problems of environmental overload, and nearly catastrophic operations of high technology are the catchwords that have penetrated public consciousness by way of the mass media.[9]

For Habermas, this diffusion of pessimistic consciousness has a number of worrying consequences. At an intellectual level, it lends weight to radical critiques of the project of modernity which abandon collective efforts to establish a good and just society. He believes this "new obscurity" also makes room for a cynicism and complacency that encourages conservative and reactionary political programmes. The end result, in Habermas's view, is that unnecessary suffering and inequality become justifiable.

Nonetheless, hopes persist that suffering will be significantly reduced through historical time. They are expressed in, for example, the optimistic scenarios surrounding the human genome project. Recognition of the ambivalence of progress, though, is also evident—in this case, it is acknowledged that while many sicknesses and diseases may be alleviated, the cures could create unanticipated side effects and, in the meantime, practices such as genetic discrimination might arise. The balance of hope and despair may be difficult to compute and probably varies. Contemporary intellectual controversies do seem to be conditioned, however, by a broad context of disappointed expectations about the historical elimination of suffering. What is the proper light in which these disappointments should be viewed? Habermas is convinced we must reconstruct an intellectual framework in which the idea of historical progress is sustained. Is this necessary, though, in order to ward off a politics that is insensitive to suffering and injustice? Are there other intellectual and political alternatives? In the next section, Habermas's proposal is outlined briefly before the remainder of the chapter considers some of the objections and alternatives to it.

Habermas's Reconstruction of Progressive Ideals

Habermas argues that the "relation of history to reason remains constitutive for the discourse of modernity—for better or worse."[10] His aim is to find a middle path between the earlier, naive views of progress and the various historicist, poststructuralist, and postmodernist critiques of the philosophy of history. Habermas admits that progress, insofar as it can be identified, is neither linear nor automatic. But he is insistent that built into history is a logic of "learning processes" that allow us to improve our habits of thought and action in the light of past mistakes. This third way involves looking for "patterns . . . in historical events [which] yield encoded indications of unfinished, interrupted, and misguided processes of self-formation that transcend the subjective consciousness of the individual."[11] It seeks to defend the idea that, in the course of history, there is a gradual sedimentation of "objective" or "congealed" virtue in social and political institutions.

For Habermas, this objective virtue grows over time and provides a threshold of learning able to withstand the variability and continual destruction of subjective experience. He claims that faith in modernity disappears only when this progressive threshold is ignored by a one-dimensional perspective. Some critics tend to reduce modern institutions to an expansion in instrumental control over nature, society, and self. Habermas's defense consists, essentially, of a distinction between the "instrumental" and "communicative" dimensions of reason that clarifies the nature of two different forms of historical progress. The key differences can be explained via a discussion of concepts such as autonomy, freedom, and responsibility. The *instrumental* application of reason, argues Habermas, involves intelligent adaptation and the pursuit of goals in the context of a contingent environment. It connotes an idea of "autonomy" as the mastery of one's surroundings. A person is "responsible" when they are able to select appropriate and efficient means to achieve predefined ends. These concepts take on a different meaning in a *communicative* context. They then entail an expansion of "the scope for unconstrained coordination of actions and consensual resolutions of conflicts."[12] From this point of view, a person is "responsible" and "autonomous" when they can subordinate and defer their own plans of action and enter a discussion that makes those plans dependent on agreement with others. Collective institutions and broad cultural patterns can be similarly interpreted, as enabling of these different kinds of freedom.

Habermas maintains that the breakdown of traditional ways of life provides modernity with an opportunity to develop both forms of freedom to a hitherto unprecedented extent. Because thought and action are determined less and less by unquestionable norms and values, they can be rationalized along either instrumental or communicative lines. Habermas argues the project of modernity, properly understood, implies a form of development in which communicative freedoms have priority and balance and "steer" instrumental forms of control. He outlines two broad processes that tend to undermine this ideal trajectory. First, in the material dimension of existence, improvements in the power and efficiency of the production process point to a release of human beings from burdensome conditions of labor. However, the uncontrolled growth of "systemic complexity" retracts this freedom through what Habermas calls a "colonization of the lifeworld": the forceful imposition of instrumental values and criteria on communicative practices. Second, in the cultural dimension of existence, the aforementioned dissolution of fixed worldviews opens up to free and conscious deliberation, the question of how we should live together. Such processes of cultural rationalization are, nevertheless, vulnerable to fragmentation that undermines any harmonious system of criteria for evaluation and decision making. With this, individuals are overwhelmed rather than freed, paralyzed by a number of equally compelling standards for thought and action. In Max Weber's words, "What is hard for modern man, and especially for the younger generation, is to measure up to an everyday life of this kind."[13]

Habermas's theory of modernity aims to clarify these processes and indicate the possibilities for further developing the progressive rather than reactionary potentials. It emphasizes the need, first, to prevent further colonization of the lifeworld by empowering free and open processes of communication in public spheres that can then steer market and state power; and, second, to defend modern cultural pluralism and the communicative freedom it enables against the twin pressures of the disintegration, and fundamentalist reassertion, of meaning. Habermas suggests this elucidation of the ambivalent promise of modernity puts a proper light on the variety of groups, classes, and movements that are struggling over these issues.[14] It also allows an identification of the extent to which particular struggles are either progressive or regressive. Thus, the issues involve what has been called the "new politics," in which the main concern is with "defending and restoring endangered ways of life" rather than with "compensations that the welfare state can provide."[15] The groups, movements, and scenes include the antinuclear and environmental movements, the peace movement, single-issue and local movements, various minorities, the psychoscene, religious fundamentalism, the tax-protest movement, school protests, the women's movement, and the movements for autonomy and independence throughout the world.[16] And the degree to which these struggles are emancipatory can be gauged by whether they seek, on the one hand, to defend "traditional or social rank" or, on the other hand, to establish ways of life emerging from "a rationalized life-world" that experiment with "new ways of cooperating and living together."[17]

From this survey of Habermas's theory of modernity, it becomes evident that his reconceptualization of the philosophy of history in terms of communications theory also has implications for the issue of agency. Since Marx, critical theory has been concerned to find an addressee or agent capable of activating the potential of modernity. It first looked to the working class or proletariat. For this reason, the failure of the working class became a preoccupation of the attempt to understand why modern societies had not turned out to be free and emancipated and whether another subject/s could take its place or complement it. Habermas's shift to communications theory reduces the intensity of these debates by claiming that no single subject, or even subjects, can or should be the addressee of critical theory. His approach identifies only potentials and ambiguities that face individuals and groups generally rather than placing responsibility on any particular agent for providing a historical guarantee. This moves the practical concern of critical theory away from a search for a particular *agent* to an analysis of the *issues* at stake in the possibility of progress.[18] From such an identification of issues, the question of *who* is interested in *what* kind of change and *why* can be broached more objectively and empirically.[19]

This does not mean that agency ceases to be a concern of Habermasian critical theory. Because the fundamental idea of history as progress is still essential, it is important, if this idea is to be practical, that theory identify situations that routinely produce, in individuals and groups, an interest in radical action and change. In particular, theory needs to locate a certain dynamic of suffering. Suffering, from this point of view, is a significant and necessary precondition of growth and progress. As Habermas argues, "the interest inherent in the pressure of suffering is also . . . an interest in enlightenment."[20] Learning generally occurs through "negative" experiences since only these experiences bring about a motivation to change. Situations in modern social and political space in which this dynamic of suffering may exist can be thought of as "litmus tests" of the potential of modernity. They are like experimental trials, giving feedback to critical commentators on whether modernity does indeed contain a unique potential for historical progression. The next section of this chapter examines such a situation and the feedback it provides: the adolescent crisis.

Modernity and the Adolescent Crisis

Habermas's interest in the adolescent crisis derived from research into the nature and significance of youth dissent and protest in the late 1960s and early

1970s. He drew on the work of, among others, Kenneth Keniston. Keniston referred to the period of extended adolescence or youth, lasting much longer than the period of puberty characteristic of earlier historical periods, as a "new stage of life."[21] He defined it as a "limbo between adolescence and adulthood" which "barely existed a century ago" but "is now universally accepted as an inherent part of the human condition."[22] He noted that education, in particular, contributed to the open-ended nature of this stage of life in which the transition from childhood to adulthood ceased to be routine or automatic. It leaves a "growing minority" of individuals without clear answers to the questions that help structure a stable adulthood: "questions of relationship to the existing society; questions of vocation; questions of social role and life style."[23] Keniston observed that a similar period of questioning and uncertainty characterized exemplary figures of history who broke through social conventions and introduced a universal moral outlook. He speculated that for the first time, substantial proportions of a generation would seek genuine freedom and independence rather than merely accept their cultural surroundings. Thus, the production of a Socrates, a Jesus, or a Gandhi might become more routine.[24] The preconditions could materialize, thought Keniston, capable of supporting a fundamental change, overcoming the "psychological ballast that [had] prevented most revolutions from doing more than reinstating the *ancien régime* in new guise."[25]

Habermas agreed that the adolescent crisis could well be a social spark capable of igniting a gradual but radical transformation—even though his hopes were typically restrained and ambivalent.[26] He referred, on the one hand, to evolutionary cultural developments that provide an environment favorable to a postconventional resolution of the crisis of adolescence. These developments mean, in principle, values and norms can now be justified only through communicative practices, practices that have built into them ideals of autonomy and freedom. Habermas postulated that insofar as this cultural configuration affects "typical socialization processes," youth would acquire a detachment from imposed "patterns of interpretation."[27] Such detachment creates a space in which questions of identity can be worked out independently and against the pressures of the political-economic system. This system encourages syndromes of "civil privatism" and "familial-occupational privatism," dispositions that promote a withdrawal from political participation in the political public sphere and a sublimation of energy into private, competitive pursuits.[28] They sustain ideologies of achievement within the educational and occupational systems and, therefore, contradict the new potentials for autonomous identity-formation. The emergence of a generation that refuses to conform in this way, thought Habermas, could sow the seeds of meaningful social change.

On the other hand, Habermas admitted an extended period of crisis might prove too burdensome for the adolescent. This undesirable alternative consists of various forms of alienation and psychological maladjustment to a condition of potential freedom. The individual, in this scenario, is left stranded between social expectations he or she no longer finds satisfying and an alternative that appeals to more expansive ideals of self-fulfillment but is out of reach. This unbearable situation, without being resolved postconventionally, must eventually lead to either a resigned absorption into the existing sphere of conventionality or a permanently alienated consciousness. Both alternatives are summed up in Fromm's phrase: "escape from freedom."[29]

What, then, do the last thirty or more years, since theorists like Keniston presented their views, indicate in relation to these alternative scenarios? This chapter does not present an exhaustive study of the theoretical and empirical material relevant to answering this question. It does, however, offer an interpretation, drawn mainly from an Australian context, that is supported by some of the evidence. This line of interpretation suggests any expectations that a greater proportion of upcoming generations would develop a postconventional moral consciousness and provide effective opposition to the modern capitalist order have largely dissolved. It submits the adolescent crisis is most likely to result in either a conventional resolution—the adoption of privatistic, consumerist, and other materialist attitudes conducive to social reproduction—or an alienated form of consciousness, unable to resolve the conflicts between social expectation and individual aspiration.[30] This view indicates the dynamic of suffering hoped for by critical theory has not eventuated in this particular case.[31]

Evidence for a growth in the alienated form of consciousness is contained in a significant body of empirical research that outlines a noticeable deterioration in the mental health and well-being of young people in Australia. A recent report by the Australian Institute of Health and Welfare found the "major burden of disease for this age group [12–24 years] is from mental disorders."[32] Mental disorders, it claimed, account for 74 percent of the noncommunicable disease burden and 55 percent of the total burden in young people.[33] Moreover, the incidence of mental disorders reaches its peak, among the population as a whole, in the eighteen- to twenty-four-years age group.[34] The report stated that concern about the psychological health of young people exists throughout the Western world:

> There appears to be evidence that the mental health problems among young people are increasing. A comprehensive study conducted in Europe suggests that over the last 50 years there has been an increase in many mental disorders occurring in young people. Studies in New Zealand have also shown increases in mental health problems among young people. It seems likely that a similar situation exists in Australia. Certainly the youth suicide rate has increased substantially over the last few decades and clear relationships between suicide and mental health problems have been demonstrated.[35]

The disproportionate burden of mental health problems carried by youth reflect wider stresses and strains being imposed on society as a whole. A 1999 Mental Health Report focused on depression concluded that the "remarkable progress in physical and material well-being for most Australians has not necessarily been matched by gains in mental and subjective well-being."[36] It found mental disorders now form a substantial part of the burden of disease in Australia. This signifies a worldwide trend that points to a continuing rise in "neuropsychiatric disorders," such that depression is projected to constitute the largest share of the burden of disease in the developing world and the second-largest worldwide by the year 2020.[37]

Once again, while any explanation of this phenomenon must be a complex one, I would like to consider one causal factor of some importance: youth perceptions of the future. Richard Eckersley, an Australian social analyst, has spent considerable time trying to understand the concrete mental processes behind the destructive behavioral patterns of some young people. His research highlights *youth's fears of the future* as a central factor.[38] Eckersley points out that young children, when prompted to express their views about the future, indicate they are affected, from an earlier and earlier age, with the feeling they can do little or nothing to alter what they consider to be the destructive society in which they live. Their views are often bleak and despairing. While it seems they are "optimistic about their personal future, expecting to get what they want out of life," he notes they "have become increasingly pessimistic about the future of their nation, humanity, the world."[39] Eckersley's reasoning is that these negative expectations have a more or less subtle effect on decisions about how to live. In general, they lead to a condition of anxiety and fear, the pressure of which creates demands for escapes, distractions, and instant gratification rather than a lifestyle involving a patient and persistent attempt to achieve freedom and independence. When coupled with a poor outlook about one's personal future, obvious forms of self-destructive behavior result, such as suicide, drug and alcohol abuse, physical violence, and crime. In other cases, where there is a positive outlook about personal success, less obvious forms of escape may still take place that betray a linkage with the broader sense of despair.[40] These more acceptable escapes involve the cultivation of negative attitudes conducive to the reproduction of a thoroughly depoliticized, capitalist society: materialism, consumerism, cynicism, short-termism, and a general irritability and intolerance in the search for a privatized version of self-fulfillment.

The subtle and less measurable escapes are particularly significant. They indicate the adolescent dynamics of suffering often work in a direction opposite to that hoped for by critical theory: suffering is helpful for the pursuit of superficial and nonemancipatory forms of progress. A society oriented around measures of development such as economic growth, technological innovation, as well as considerations of national honor and party-political prestige may even have a vested interest in intensifying rather than easing this suffering.[41] Greater economic growth, for example, implies a faster-paced lifestyle, which compresses the time and space available to youth for reflection on their conduct of life and compels them, instead, to merely fit in and conform to an existing structure. In short, the sense of desperation characteristic of the experience of hopelessness promotes unhealthy behavioral patterns that are actually conducive to a conventional and materialist agenda of progress. This indicates that the differences between conventional and alienated ways of life may even be narrowed down into variations on a single phenomenon.

Rethinking Progress

Eckersley claims the bleak visions of the future held by young people

> represent a loss of faith in the central tenet of Western culture: the belief in progress, in the continuing betterment of human life. It denies young people, who are establishing their identities, values and sense of place, a social ideal to believe in—something to convince them to subordinate their own selfish interest to a higher social goal.[42]

Habermas, whose critical theory anticipates problems with freedom and meaning in modern life, has been similarly concerned with this loss of faith. He has sought to reconstruct an idea of progress that can restore confidence and address the problems leading from a more or less explicit despair about the future. The question posed here, though, is whether a resurrection of the continuum of progress is a desirable response. I argue it is not and that it is necessary to rethink ideals of progress more fundamentally. This final section of the chapter indicates further why a revitalized belief in progress may be counterproductive and what alternative approaches are possible.

It has been argued, thus far, that a sense of scarcity conditions the conventional and alienated outcomes of the crisis of adolescence. The particular concern here is with scarcity in its cultural sense and how the degree of meaning in life is influenced by different forms of historical consciousness. The modern consciousness of history, however revised or modified, may well exacerbate cultural scarcity even as it promises to diminish it. Modern identity is shaped strongly by the ideal of progress and yet, for individuals and groups, the expectations created are often continually disappointed. If the ideal of progress is reinstated, this logic is maintained: "progressive" attempts to address and ease suffering actually generate suffering. Certainly, the fear, anxiety, and despair of youth, and of individuals generally, in the face of a bleak future need to be recognized, responded to, and relieved. This is necessary for any effort at redirecting the antisocial and self-destructive behavior that otherwise results. But propping up the lingering belief in progress may only intensify expectations, produce false hopes, and lead to even greater disaffection.

A way out of this struggle between hope and despair is evident in alternative conceptions of history. Löwith observes that in the ancient Greek and early Christian worldviews, hope and despair were recognized as "evils" that go together. From this point of view, an historical consciousness dominated by the waxing and waning of future expectations is too subjective and too partisan. The implication is that a more objective and desirable approach involves rising above history by withdrawing the emotional investments placed in it. This outlook recommends an attitude in which there is a peculiar combination of skepticism and faith as opposed to periodic wavering between hope and despair. It is characterized by the "wisdom" that it is "hopeless to look forward to better times in the future, since there is hardly a future which, when it has become present, does not disappoint. Man's hopes are 'blind,' i.e., unintelligent and miscalculating, deceptive, and illusory."[43] Learning from history means to accustom oneself to endure it cheerfully and with dignity. Thus, Greek reflection about history had no need to go further than the belief that individuals have the "resourcefulness to meet every situation with magnanimity."[44]

Hannah Arendt makes a similar point in her drawing on the ancient Greeks. The modern historical outlook, she argues, is inherently destructive of meaning because it conceives meaning as an end to be brought about. More specifically, it is destructive because of an inability to distinguish between means and ends. The notion of progress through time implies that "every attained end" is changed "immediately into the means to a new end," so that in a world of "seemingly unending progress" each "aim of today becomes the means of a better tomorrow."[45] For Arendt, the attempt to consciously and intentionally create freedom and meaning is futile because it leads from a misunderstanding of the human condition. The modern philosophy of history thus extends and enhances precisely what needs to be questioned, doubted, overcome—an instrumental conception of the road to happiness. It implies an acceptance of untutored and uneducated values and priorities, encouraging conformity and convention rather than freedom and independence. Put differently, the underlying currents of fear and insecurity in the face of uncertainty are "radicalized" rather than overcome by assurances about a better future in which the vagaries of history will be eliminated.[46] The demand for progressive meaning, in this perspective, reflects an anxious preoccupation with one's place in the world. Modernity has, as a whole, been guilty of this insofar as it has sought to think of itself as having universal significance, of standing at or near the end of a historical development that gives it a superior perspective over all other times and places. For this reason, modern culture, in inflating itself to absolute proportions, risks an undignified death.[47]

Habermas's distinction between communicative and instrumental rationality *within* a philosophy of progress is, therefore, insufficient because it is still too tainted with instrumental overtones. A better approach, it is argued, would encourage individuals to free themselves from the illusion of historical progress, to become more independent of the vagaries of historical change. It suggests a certain indifference to, and detachment from, worldly events as a precondition of individual autonomy. This perspective seeks to contain suffering in the face of historical contingency and brutality rather than transpose it into a desire for certainty and security. Such a form of self-reflection, which stands back from history, encourages a sympathy with the ancient focus on the virtues.[48] The practice of the virtues cultivates character traits that protect individuals from projecting fears and desires onto the outside world. It allows them, instead, to question their existing economy of needs and wants and see whether these can or should be reorganized in order to live well. The emphasis is on questioning and overcoming the reduction of history to a human framework of will and desire. A progressive philosophy of history, on the other hand, tends to rigidify the human being and sanction only what exists and its further elaboration.[49]

To be sure, a nonprogressive conception of history is faced with a number of difficulties in contemporary circumstances. As already discussed, the dualistic structure of much political thought and practice presupposes that a mean-spirited, conservative politics gains legitimacy when a progressive mentality declines. Given the contemporary enthusiasm for "third ways," though, it seems reasonable to rethink progress aloud for the sake of going beyond what are false alternatives. Otherwise, progressive beliefs become merely compulsive, thoughtless reactions to conservative approaches. Moreover, they render themselves insensitive to their own destructive impact. To paraphrase William Connolly, the drive to be progressive contains too many liabilities because it renders people less able to adjust positively to inevitable disappointments and disruptions.[50] Paradoxically, this drive lends support to conservatives who are only too willing to point out the impracticality of Enlightenment ideals when the future appears limited. Stubborn attachment to progressive standards for critique of actually existing societies could even mean that "generic cynicism is at risk of becoming the defining mark of the sophisticated left."[51] Thus, while there are dangers in questioning progress and in recognizing the limits of politics, it is also dangerous to allow debates to continue along conventional lines.[52]

Like adolescence, then, modernity is marked by a consciousness fueled with hopes for freedom and independence in the future. It should be remembered, however, the very question of whether there is a progressive meaning to history has itself been brought about, and made important, *historically*. There were times when this question had no place. In turn, the sense of meaninglessness and despair occupying the present mind, particularly the adolescent mind, may have an air of legitimacy only because of the persisting assumption of historical meaning. The recognition of a significant mental health problem in modern societies, particularly among young people, demonstrates more than ever that improvements in science, technology, and even legal, juridical, and moral structures do not entail, necessarily, more human happiness or well-being. Perhaps some of these improvements even depend on the maintenance of a threshold of suffering and unease.

We may be experiencing a hangover from a lengthy romance with Enlightenment dreams, dreams that are just one expression of that seemingly primordial demand for the universe to be structured in accordance with human needs and preferences. But there are possibilities outside a horizon of thinking in which meaning depends on a logic of historical progress. As Jane Bennett points out, a sense of attachment to the world and experiences of wonder and enchantment do not require a belief in inherent meaning, whether of a teleological or theological kind.[53] It is precisely this assumption that needs to be questioned for the sake of an individuality shaped by aesthetic concerns, an individuality still able to love the world after purposive metaphysical designs have disintegrated.

Such considerations do not indicate that we can or should do without notions of progress. Meaning often derives, at both the individual and collective levels of existence, from working toward the achievement of clear aims and goals.[54] The suggestion is, rather, that we need to think more deeply about how, where, and why we would like to progress. A lazy, ideological emphasis on progress tends to sustain the validity of the present configuration of social and political values and interests, a configuration not necessarily conducive to the satisfaction of basic human needs and aspirations. Efforts to think and act more concretely in regard to our hopes for the future, a willingness to question ideals of progress without drawing mean-spirited conclusions, and an openness to possibilities for nonpurposive forms of meaning may help dismantle the destructive dynamics and politics of suffering evident today.

3

Dogmatic Retreats and Skeptical Adventures

One of the central dynamos behind progress in modernity has been the tendency to criticize. Kant claimed "[o]ur age is the genuine age of criticism, to which everything must submit,"[1] while a contemporary Kantian declares that all of our naive certainties have been "drawn into a dynamic of problematization that no one today can elude."[2] If ideas about progress have an ambiguous value, as argued in the previous chapter, what is the role and value of criticism in reforming and improving ethical and political life? How should criticism be directed, regulated, and disciplined, if at all? Should we develop some kinds of criticism rather than others? How one responds to these questions is symptomatic of the approach one adopts in dealing with the aftereffects of knowledge.

This chapter identifies a characteristic which, from the point of view of the requirements of individuality, helps distinguish productive from counterproductive forms of criticism. Two different conceptions of the relationship between nature and culture, it is asserted, make possible corresponding forms of critical practice. A distinction between nature and culture is usually thought to be a condition of possibility of criticism. The idea is that, in comparison to natural laws, norms and conventions are merely relative and, therefore, susceptible to criticism and change. The chapter contests this view and argues criticism is still possible when nature and culture are seen to be continuous with one another. It is important to note the claim is that criticism undertaken in the context of this sense of continuity between nature and culture is more valuable for attempts to cultivate individuality.

The chapter develops a general contrast between "dogmatic" and "skeptical" modes of criticism. It begins with a discussion of Plato's reservations about promoting philosophical criticism of moral and ethical values. For Plato, critical reflection must be regulated firmly so as to encourage a genuine sense of skepticism rather than promote a reckless disregard for moral restraints. He suggests that criticism is all too easily mobilized by unquestioned desires and needs, thus becoming rather counterproductive in its applications. A similar concern with disciplining criticism is present in the work of many contemporary theorists, even if they do not reach the rather paternalistic conclusions of Plato. The second part of the chapter considers the approaches to criticism developed by Jürgen Habermas and Judith Butler. These theorists think the critical spirit of modern culture is desirable but they seek to shape and direct it in particular ways. It is contended, however, that these thinkers, while different in many ways, both develop a counterproductive and dogmatic mode of criticism on the basis of a distinction between nature and culture.

After outlining an alternative and more productive critical method in connection with Stephen White's notion of "weak ontology," the third and final part of the chapter draws on the work of Nietzsche and the ancient skeptics. It reconstructs their reasons for thinking that the distinction between nature and culture, often held to be a condition of possibility for criticism, actually subverts a skeptical and productive style of critical practice. It is also argued that while this skeptical form of criticism seems to have conservative implications, it may represent a better understanding of how desirable ethical and political change can take place.

The Dangers of Dialectic

In a section of the *Republic* dealing with the education of philosopher kings, there is a discussion about the dangers of philosophy or of "dialectic."[3] Dialectic is a process involving reflection on premises at the basis of received knowledge. It contrasts with other disciplines such as mathematics that teach students to reason within a framework of accepted assumptions. The practice of dialectic tends to corrode the corpus of belief that, until now, was used unproblematically to interpret and understand the world. It brings about an awareness of ignorance, an ignorance once masked by the certainty with which ideas and assertions were entertained. Dialectic leads one to see that what previously appeared to be genuine knowledge is actually mere opinion. The student realizes how careless they have been in accepting and adopting the attitudes and ideas of others. This process is a prerequisite of both freedom and valid knowledge. Socrates cautions, though, that introducing the study of dialectic or the art of questioning too early in the educational process can have counterproductive results. While dialectic is essential, not everyone can readily access its potential benefits. He maintains that only after a lengthy and rigorous process of physical and intellectual education will it become possible to identify the privileged few with an "aptitude for dialectic."[4]

The issues involved are considered in a dialogue between Socrates and Glaucon when the former asks, "Haven't you noticed the appalling harm done by dialectic at present?"[5] Socrates has observed that the art of questioning often promotes attitudes of arrogance and insensitivity rather than inducing humility and an awareness of one's ignorance. He points out its effect can be to "fill people with indiscipline."[6] The distinction implied here, which marks out those suitable from those unsuitable for philosophy, is between students interested in worldly concerns and those who look beyond the attractions of money, power, and sensual pleasure. When worldly attractions have the upper hand in the person's outlook on life, critical reflection merely weakens the powers of restraint. Reflection creates doubts about tradition but fails to penetrate further into the nature of desire. The educational process, if it is not to encourage such dangerous implications, must first aim to bring out the natural aptitudes of students in order to find out the path most appropriate to each. Since the art of questioning may lead in either a worldly or otherworldly direction, it is important to identify early on those few individuals able to be future philosopher kings. For the others, the ideal republic will channel their creativity in a way that substitutes philosophical discipline with more suitable ways of life.

In the absence of an ideal political structure, nonetheless, the philosophical art is abused. As Socrates explains, a process of corruption rather than education then takes place. In childhood, he says, the strength of tradition disciplines the individual, regulating their egoism within a framework. At this stage, the individual is a creature of convention, inheriting the knowledge of what is right and wrong. Out of respect and reverence, the child identifies with the way of life of its parents. Even if the individual is attracted to "habits of an opposite kind, which have a deceitful attraction because of the pleasures they offer,"[7] respect maintains discipline and a stable, steady outlook. The art of questioning, however, tends to lessen the power of tradition. For when the child is introduced to discussions about traditions and values, they are easily "refuted in argument."[8] And when this experience takes place repeatedly, "he is driven to think that there's no difference between honorable and disgraceful, and so on with all the other values, like right and good, that he used to revere."[9] It dawns on him or her that there is a distinction between nature and convention, that social mores and norms possess an arbitrary quality. With this, the individual gains a certain degree of intellectual freedom and detachment from powerful ideals and beliefs. Without any other direction, though, this freedom easily falls prey to another unquestioned way of life. The immensely attractive alternative, given that the individual's egoism has merely been restrained rather than understood, is to give free reign to the push and pull of pleasure and the desire for gratification. As the hold of tradition declines, it becomes easier to justify the pursuit of pleasure and avoidance of pain as the best way to live. Thus, Socrates asks, "When he's lost any respect or feeling for his former beliefs but not yet found the truth, where is he likely to turn? Won't it be to a life which flatters his desires?"[10]

Socrates practised dialectic with many of the young people in classical Athens. Plato is probably drawing attention here to the apparently harmful effects this practice had on some of those youths. Without discipline, in this way of seeing things, only the pleasures are left as motives for action: anything goes and anything can be justified. It was in this context that Plato mounted his critique of the "sophists." The sophists also drew attention to the distinction between nature and convention to emphasize that the moral and social fabric is not preordained but merely a historical product. Their interest, though, was not to stimulate a pursuit of philosophical truth. Rather, they communicated this insight in order to help aspiring politicians gain power and prestige in the polis. If one is aware that all arguments are equally ungrounded, it becomes easier to manipulate a discussion to make one's own position look stronger. To protect the reputation of philosophy against this illegitimate use Plato, through the voice of Socrates, stresses that dialectic must be handled carefully in the educational process as a whole: "All we've been saying has been said in the attempt to ensure that only men of steady and disciplined character shall be admitted to philosophic discussions, and not anyone, however unqualified, as happens at present."[11]

As the premises of this book imply, it is rather academic to draw such distinctions in contemporary circumstances. Criticism and questioning are no longer entitlements but pervasive cultural practices. While dialectic may once have been the privilege of the few, it must now only be the few who manage to avoid the tendency to reflect and doubt. Not unlike Plato, Alasdair MacIntyre laments this situation. He argues the absence in the "contemporary conventional curriculum" of any positive and defensible contribution to an understanding of what morality is explains why "the teaching of ethics is so often destructive and skeptical in its effects on the minds of those taught."[12] But if Bernard Williams is correct to say "there is no route back from reflectiveness"[13] how might we regulate and manage our modern habit of criticism? Which forms of criticism are better than others? In the next section of the chapter, I would like to reconsider a debate about these questions, a debate that illustrates a generally unproductive understanding of the role and value of criticism.

Dogmatic Retreats: Habermas and Butler

Jürgen Habermas and Judith Butler are at odds about the role criticism should play in connection with the conduct of progressive, democratic politics. One aim of this section of the chapter is to outline briefly the nature of their disagreement. The other aim is to demonstrate that they have something in common which, to a significant degree, overshadows their differences: a kind of dogmatic sensibility. Both Habermas and Butler, it is claimed, share an anxiety about the potentially destructive effects criticism has on their political projects. The suggestion is put forward that while each theorist strongly endorses a critical approach to questions of truth, morality, and value more generally, they both limit and regulate criticism in a counterproductive way.

To begin with Habermas, he argues a form of basic differentiation between nature and culture makes criticism possible. It is only with what he refers to as the "differentiation of world from lifeworld" or the "linguistification of the sacred" that worldviews can be viewed as different from the world itself, as *interpretations* susceptible to criticism.[14] For Habermas, however, this is only the first of three stages in the critical posture of modernity.[15] For while worldviews that incorporate the difference between nature and culture are more enlightened, they are still subject to suspicion. "Ideology critique" enters the scene as a second phase of critical reflection. Here, doubt focuses on theoretical assertions whose validity rests on the power of social and political interests. The critique of ideology is sensitive to the way specific individuals and groups benefit from the dominance of particular ways of viewing the world. Just as the structures of modern consciousness allow us to see clearly how traditional worldviews gained a false credibility by being woven in with traditional ways of life, the critique of ideology discloses how modern worldviews often reflect and stabilize the unequal power relations of the social order. For Habermas, the critique of ideology advances enlightenment by raising it to a higher level of reflection: enlightenment attains awareness of itself through reflecting on the validity of its own products.

Nonetheless, the development of criticism is still not finished. A third stage emerges when enlightenment attains what Habermas calls a "second-order reflectiveness." Here, "ideology critique *itself* comes under suspicion of not producing (any more) truths."[16] The previously unquestioned standards of this mode of critique are held to be nonuniversal in character, reflecting merely the structures of a modern, bourgeois society. Habermas accepts the cogency of this observation. He acknowledges the bourgeois version of critique was unproblematic only insofar as its ideals contradicted the reality it supported. Thus, critics needed only to confront actors and institutions with the contrast between their standards and their practice. The infusion of ideals within institutions functioned as a "utopian potential" that transcended and negated the existing reality. Habermas maintains it was on this basis that a "second generation of ideologies" grew up in modernity, such as anarchism, communism, socialism, and fascism.[17]

But if criticism goes further to question any and all standards, then the "suspicion of ideology becomes *total*."[18] It is at this point in Habermas's work, I think, that an underlying dogmatism emerges most clearly. For he insists there are universal and justifiable standards of criticism. Modern structures of consciousness, in his view, are the result of an evolutionary process and contain a universal potential for enlightenment. Habermas concedes knowledge and belief should be treated skeptically, but he believes in disciplining criticism within the parameters of the "communicatively rational" fabric of human life.

> Ultimately, there is only one criterion by which beliefs can be judged valid, and that is that they are based on agreement reached by argumentation. This means that *everything* whose validity is at all disputable rests on shaky foundations. It matters little if the ground underfoot shakes a bit less for those who debate problems of physics than for those who debate problems of morals and aesthetics. The difference is a matter of degree only. . . .[19]

Habermas hopes to bring what seems to be an endless process of critical dissolution to an end, placing communicative rationality as the last stop beyond which skepticism cannot go.

Habermas's argument against radical skepticism reaches its climax with his claim about "performative contradiction." Skeptics, he argues, seek to detach themselves from life and look on as casual observers, disinterested in what is at stake in everyday action and interaction. It is true, and also very desirable, says Habermas, that we take such a nonperformative or "hypothetical" attitude toward particular ideas or systems of ideas that have been isolated from the totality of social life. The great virtue of modern culture is that it provides us with an opportunity to be detached, by setting aside the pressures of everyday action, and learn through discourse. We are then able, in principle, to reach a mutual understanding about specific propositions and beliefs, based only on the "unforced force of the better argument." But this is quite different, he declares, from the skeptical position that would like to systematize the hypothetical attitude and use it to reflect on life as a whole. Habermas insists that "[i]ndividuals who have been socialized cannot take a hypothetical attitude towards the form of life and the personal life history that have shaped their own identity."[20] While one can doubt in the particular, it is impossible to doubt universally.

Habermas suggests the "skeptic who sees in advance that he will be caught in [such] performative contradictions will reject the game of wits from the outset."[21] That is, rather than trying to prove his position, which implies raising claims to validity and participating in life, the consistent skeptic will ignore the argumentative game and adopt a "dropout posture."[22] More significantly, such a posture may become widespread and undermine democratic political culture. For Habermas, such antidemocratic tendencies "infiltrate everyday consciousness by way of the educational system" and "[u]nder extreme conditions they can contribute to the moral disarmament of academics already in the grip of a cultivated skepticism."[23]

"What is at stake," says Habermas, "is Western culture's confidence in itself."[24] A conviction held particularly by those on the left of politics is being shaken: the belief that recognition of a bedrock of truth binds us all in a collective project of emancipation. He argues that if the rational, universal structure of modernity is ignored, the door is opened to a variety of conservative agendas, such as the restoration of traditional values or unregulated capitalist development. It is crucial, for him, to provide theoretical grounds for resisting such reactionary political programs. In other words, it is important to preserve a distinction between myth and enlightenment, between nature and culture. Habermas admits that while any *particular* convention or norm can always be denaturalized, exposed as cultural and rendered susceptible to criticism and change, it is natural and unavoidable for human beings to live in some kind of culture. At the transcendental level, culture *is* nature: "There is no form of sociocultural life that is not at least implicitly geared to maintaining communicative action by means of argument."[25] Habermas's theory is meant to explain why engaging in communicative and deliberative democratic action is both necessary and unavoidable. And while he admits these claims may sound dogmatic, they are, he says, "'dogmatic' only in a harmless sense."[26]

Other theorists have been less worried about the perceived dangers of relativism, as the difference between nature and culture seems to disappear. Rather than dam up criticism, they have preferred to let it run its course. Judith Butler, for example, would like to unleash the skeptical momentum flowing from the radicalized critique of ideology. She argues that the methodological demand "[t]o expose the contingent acts that create the appearance of a naturalistic necessity" has been felt at least since Marx.[27] But she wishes to take things further by mobilizing innovations in this tradition of suspicion, such as Foucault's procedure of "genealogy" and Derrida's method of "deconstruction." For Butler, these more recent approaches are useful precisely because they unsettle the very motivations supporting the critical impulse. We can no longer be content, she claims, with a critique of ideology that intends to question norms that, by being naturalized, have restricted the freedom of subjects. Rather, we must go further and question the *nature* of subjectivity itself. Nevertheless, I believe a theoretical movement similar to the one just described with respect to Habermas dominates Butler's work. While she follows the path of criticism further than him, she too appears to think a last-minute dogmatism is necessary to sustain radical change.

On the one hand, then, Butler insists the postulation of a "before," "outside," or "beyond" of subjectivity or power is both a "cultural impossibility" and a "politically impracticable dream."[28] In an explanatory sense, she pursues a Nietzschean critique of "the metaphysics of substance," intent on exposing how grammatical conventions are turned into statements about "reality." This critique, in Butler's view, deconstructs "the very notion of the psychological person as a substantive thing."[29] The "I" that accompanies our thoughts and actions refers not to an ontological order but merely sustains illusions about the locus of control and responsibility in our lives. Politically speaking, Butler maintains the employment of the subject as foundation has limited the possibilities of progressive struggle. Her arguments often apply specifically to feminist and queer politics but they have a broader significance. She claims "it is no longer clear that feminist theory ought to try to settle the questions of primary identity in order to get on with the task of politics."[30] Feminists have often sought such foundations, for example Simone de Beauvoir who tried to ground critical practice "in the sexed specificity of the female body."[31] But to presume the female body as given—or anything as given and indisputable for that matter—in order to provide a starting point for practice, is to limit the possibilities of politics. More precisely, it is to circumscribe those possibilities within the very dominant regime one is seeking to subvert. The failure to theorize even the depths of nature as culturally constructed represents, in Butler's view, a specific complicity with the existing hegemony. In the case of heterosexism, for example, to treat "the materiality of sex as a given presupposes and consolidates the normative conditions of its own emergence."[32] The consequence is a compliant reformism without radical, transformative potential.

For Butler, a politics freed from ontological illusions involves "affirm[ing] identities that are alternately instituted and relinquished according to the purposes at hand."[33] Her basic political strategy is premised on a denaturalization of the categories in which we have been imprisoned so that a "performative" process of resignification—the medium of agency and freedom—can take place. And yet, such insights about subjectivity make progressive politics rather difficult. Put simply, if subjectivity is constructed all the way down, what is the point in emancipation at all if there is nothing to be freed? If there is no underlying essence of the human being to be released from political oppression, how can we sustain the progressive impulse? Progressive politics has always faced substantial difficulties, in the form of systematic external opposition by a range of conservative and reactionary forces to a freer and more egalitarian society. Now, however, with a consciousness of the illusory nature of subjectivity, this politics must come to grips with a deep-seated internal contradiction. It appears, from Butler's point of view, that the very attempt to create freedom is riddled with a violent dynamic of its own that merely multiplies and intensifies the sites of domination. For Butler, the radical critique of subjectivity amounts to a "postliberatory insight."[34]

To repeat, Butler is not afraid of pursuing this insight. Since there is no prior subject to be emancipated, in her view, identity possesses "an orginary complicity with power."[35] Our sense of being is constituted by a "primary dependency" and a "primary vulnerability," so that to have an identity at all means to be constrained.[36] "To desire the conditions of one's own subordination is," she says, "required to persist as oneself."[37] Agency and action seem to be condemned from the very beginning. A vicious circle makes up human life since "[a]ny effort to oppose . . . subordination will necessarily presuppose and reinvoke it."[38] To resist and fight also means to maintain and continue. Thoroughgoing criticism allows us to see that the desire for life itself may be a passion for grief and suffering. Nevertheless, a dogmatic strain also enters the scene of Butler's reflections at this stage, when she insists a conception of agency can still be preserved from the ruins of subjectivity. We must resist the conservative and cynical appropriation of insights about the dissolution of the subject, an appropriation which places "final responsibility" for subordination on the subordinated themselves.[39] Thus, Butler labors to find an alternative, to mark out a section of space and time able to provide us with a basis for agency and radical change. Perhaps in a way similar to the sophisticated debates about the "relative autonomy" of the state, she aims to preserve a glimmer of hope—the subject, after all, is not completely conditioned and oppressive. In a variety of formulations, she points out that a more sober and less optimistic politics of emancipation is still possible on the basis of the subject. There is scope for agency in "the hiatus in iterability," the potential for "a repetition that fails to repeat loyally."[40] While we are constrained to repeat and sustain our identities as a condition of life itself, there is room for variability and permutations.

> Power considered as a condition of the subject is necessarily not the same as power considered as what the subject is said to wield. The power that initiates the subject fails to remain continuous with the power that is the subject's agency. A significant and potentially enabling reversal occurs when power shifts from its status as a condition of agency to the subject's own agency.[41]

At this point, though, I think Butler simply reintroduces the dichotomy between the internal and the external, the natural and the cultural, that she seeks so systematically to undermine. When it all boils down, her very sophisticated account of agency has the same skeletal structure as the traditional theory of the subject: there is still an entity, even if more hedged in than previously thought, that is the source of agency.

Butler wishes to avoid the implications of her radical criticism, the idea there might be no such thing as freedom to fight for. Commentators such as Alan Schrift have argued that it may be better, for political reasons, to establish a less onerous and more straightforward foundation for emancipatory politics.[42] Schrift asks, given Butler's basic political motivations, whether it is wise to engage in such a debilitating critique of the subject. He suggests an earlier generation of French existentialists might provide superior theoretical resources:

> If the motivation behind Butler's philosophizing is ultimately political, and if her goal is ultimately emancipatory, might she do better to

> align herself with Merleau-Ponty, or to look to him for philosophico-political support rather than to Lacan or Althusser? . . . To put it bluntly, might the Left do better working with the political resources of the Merleau-Pontyan or Sartrean variety than the political versions that have emerged from France in the last thirty years? That is a question that has come increasingly to the fore as various theorists of a radical or agonal democratic politics look for intellectual resources with which to develop this political position.[43]

Whether or not Shrift is correct, he points to a dialectic at work in the theory of Butler, a dialectic also present in the writings of Habermas: a clash between dogma and critique. This dialectic, I would argue, is a rather counterproductive mode of criticism. Neither theorist seems to get beyond a wearying struggle of balancing conflicting theoretical impulses. In both cases, criticism is presumed to be essentially negative and destructive in character while a positive and constructive moment emerges only with a residual and dogmatic political commitment.

As discussed in the introduction, Stephen White has recently provided an overview of a different and, I think, more productive way of doing political theory and criticism. White speaks of a "weak ontological turn" and seeks to elaborate the meaning of this turn in connection with four of its key representatives, one of which is Butler.[44] In a moment, I will indicate why Butler may not be an appropriate theorist for White to choose but will, for now, simply outline a few of his main claims. White points out that if we accept the skeptical implications of modern criticism and feel unable to defend a strong ontology à la MacIntyre, then two other "modes of thinking" seem to exhaust the options currently available: postmodernism or poststructuralism and political liberalism.[45] He aims to demonstrate there is a better alternative, namely the weak ontological approach. It compares favorably, in his view, both with the destructive criticism of postmodernism and poststructuralism that are unable to offer a coherently affirmative account of ethics and politics, and with the thin ontology of political liberalism which is also limited in its capacity to provide affirmative orientations.[46] White argues these positions ignore the impossibility of relinquishing thick ontological conceptions and he suggests a better method is to employ such ideas in a self-consciously critical manner. Rather than be inhibited about metaphysics, he advocates a deliberate but contestable application of it.

A key point in White's account concerns the relation between theory and practice characteristic of weak ontology. He notes, in particular, how the notion of "cultivation" becomes prominent once theory mobilizes ontological conceptions without aiming primarily to justify them in cognitive fashion. Since the objective is neither to defend nor reject a truth about the world, weak ontologies have "an aesthetic-affective quality." "They disclose the world to us in such a way that we think *and* feel it differently than we might otherwise. Their appeal turns partially on how well they allow us to cope with the pressures and challenges of late modern life."[47] Theory and practice intersect, then, at the level of cultivation, in terms of "the measured pursuit of an array of related practices and self-disciplines."[48] Weak-ontological claims are not foundations but perform a "prefiguring" role, "in the sense of providing broad cognitive and affective orientation."[49] And such claims may be revised in the course of ongoing reflection and argumentation in light of the way they impact on our affective sensibilities.

To return briefly, then, to my treatment of Butler. I have indicated the overriding dynamic of her work is negative in character. Her project has an affirmative moment only because of a residual dogmatism about uncovering the truth about agency. White admits his own reading of Butler as an example of weak ontology "may seem forced in its characterization" since "negative gestures" tend to predominate in her oeuvre while her affirmations depend more on a "thin" rather than "weak" ontology. He "challenges" her to acknowledge and develop further the ontological perspective *implicit* in her writings.[50] Whether or not Butler's theorizing is of a weak-ontological kind, the point remains that to embark on a slippery slope of negative criticism safeguarded only by a thin ontology is an unproductive mode of criticism. The thinning-out strategy ignores its own ontological prefigurations and misses the opportunity to develop them in a deliberately critical but affirmative way. In the next and final section of the chapter, I would like to elaborate on a weak ontological idea that might prove to be a productive element along the path of criticism. Using theoretical fragments drawn from Nietzsche and the ancient skeptics, I will focus on how the presumption of an identity, rather than distinction, between nature and culture is a useful framework for criticism. I will also indicate its implications for ethics and politics in contrast to the typical modern ontology in which nature and culture are separated from one another.

Skeptical Adventures: Nietzsche and the Ancient Skeptics

In the work of Habermas and Butler, a distinction between nature and culture establishes the logic of criticism. As this logic proceeds the distinction is itself subject to criticism. And yet these theorists, it has been claimed, dogmatically reinstate this distinction since it is thought to be necessary for sustaining radical change. But if we consider Nietzsche's writings, to begin, it is possible to imagine a different outcome of this trajectory of criticism. Nietzsche talks of a "decisive event" and a "great separation" when one first alienates oneself, with the means of criticism, from the attachments providing for certainty, security, and identity.[51] This alienation is a tentative step toward freedom, in his view, but also a perilous breaking away that may end in disaster: "It is also a disease that can destroy man, this first outburst of strength and will to self-determination, self-valorization, this will to *free* will."[52] Criticism is essential to the development of autonomy, since unquestioned commitment to beliefs and ideas is the source of various kinds of dependency. But this skepticism also brings forth weakness and subordination, as the strength provided by attachments is lost without replacement. The hope is that "from the sickness of severe suspicion, one returns *newborn*, having shed one's skin."[53] In the initial phases of critical practice, though, there is a "morbid isolation," a "desert of . . . experimental years," which is a long way from "that enormous, overflowing certainty and health . . . that *mature* freedom of the spirit."[54] What factors are involved in determining these different implications of criticism?

As someone who has experienced both the sickness and health of a critical outlook, Nietzsche believes he is in a good position to answer such a question. In his view, one of the problems with modern culture, which explains much of its life-negating features, is the failure to consistently push criticism through to its logical conclusions. A clear, theoretical expression of this constipated criticism is provided by Schopenhauer. For Nietzsche, Schopenhauer helped clear the air of a culture polluted by an idealist, Christian heritage. Schopenhauer posed anew the question of the value of existence, setting doubt free from a belief in the divinity of existence and demanding an honest atheism.[55] But his pessimistic conclusions, according to Nietzsche, betray a continuing state of contamination. Schopenhauerian pessimism is only a first phase of atheism, a stage that must be overcome for the sake of both physiological and intellectual health:

> As we thus reject the Christian interpretation and condemn its "meaning" like counterfeit, *Schopenhauer's* question immediately comes to us in a terrifying way: *Has existence any meaning at all?* It will require a few centuries before this question can even be heard completely and in its full depth. What Schopenhauer himself said in answer to this question was—forgive me—hasty, youthful, only a compromise, a way of remaining—remaining stuck—in precisely those Christian-ascetic moral perspectives in which one had *renounced faith* along with the faith in God.[56]

Schopenhauer frees himself from Christian hypocrisy to the extent that he reports on the world as he actually sees it—"ungodly, immoral, 'inhuman.'" But he then sighs at the harshness of life due to a subtle persistence of Christian expectations, that things *should* be otherwise. Nietzsche, along with his free-spirited friends, on the other hand, "are far from claiming the world is worth *less*" because it is unjust. Since there is no other, heavenly world to redeem it, "it would seem laughable to us today if man were to insist on inventing values that were supposed to *excel* the value of the actual world."[57]

It is important to note that Nietzsche's opposition to pessimism does not mean he is an optimist: "How high above and far beyond the pitiable shallow-pated chatter about optimism contra pessimism I [have] leapt!"[58] He contrasts what he calls Schopenhauer's "romantic pessimism" not with optimism, but with "dionysian pessimism."[59] With this distinction, Nietzsche contends that he has found a genuine standard for judging human beings and cultural expressions, for differentiating, in particular, the sick, morbid, and decadent from the good, healthy, and strong. Dionysian pessimism is full of gratitude for life in spite of the immense tragedy of existence. By contrast, romantic pessimism is burdened with life, weary of existence and always seeking escape, distraction, entertainment. "Regarding all aesthetic values I now avail myself of this main distinction: I ask in every instance, 'is it hunger or superabundance that has here become creative?'"[60] The romantic hopes and imagines life could be different, suffers constantly from defeat and frustration and creates out of despair; while the dionysian takes life for what it is, finds a meaning in whatever happens and creates out of a superfluity of energy and power.

How, then, can criticism make romantic pessimism give way to a flowering of gratitude? Nietzsche suggests the way we conceive of the relationship between nature and culture is one important consideration. He makes this point when reflecting on the alternative ways of life open to the individual who, in modernity, necessarily becomes aware of the fallibility of knowledge. At first, it is likely the person will become bogged in despair once realizing the contingency of all that he has previously believed and lived for.

> All human life is sunk deep in untruth; the individual cannot pull it out of this well without growing profoundly annoyed with his entire past, without finding his present motives (like honor) senseless, and without opposing scorn and disdain to the passions that urge one on to the future and to the happiness in it.[61]

The sense of meaninglessness, and the anger at this, represent a reaction to the hypocrisy of one's upbringing and culture, surroundings in which one once belonged in good spirits. Nietzsche insists, however, an alternative reaction is possible, a completely different "aftereffect of knowledge," where the individual is prompted to free himself from the very standards of convention and social expectation to which he is now merely opposed. The person who is "mild, and basically cheerful" will not be overcome by the disintegration of cultural ideals, but perceive the joyful prospects of "the ordinary chains of life" falling from him. To be sure, the

> old motives of intense desire would still be strong at first, due to old, inherited habit, but they would gradually grow weaker under the influence of cleansing knowledge. Finally one would live among men

> and with oneself as in *nature*, without praise, reproaches, overzealousness, delighting in many things as in a spectacle that one formerly had only to fear.[62]

This idea that the cultural world might be perceived as merely an aspect of the broader natural environment is also put forward by the ancient skeptics. The ancient skeptics aimed to radically criticize the role and value of belief in human life. They sought, in particular, to free individuals from holding beliefs since cognitive or ethical commitments were held to be the main source of inward conflict, anxiety, and unhappiness.[63] In order to do this, the skeptics employed "ten modes" or patterns of argument.[64] The basic aim was to show that contradictory beliefs are equally plausible and, on seeing this, one has no option but to "suspend judgment." While the purpose of philosophy might normally be thought to involve resolving difference, the skeptic seeks to avoid being dragged into controversies among "deluded and self-satisfied dogmatists."[65] He or she evades the traditional objective of philosophical instruction, that of trying to convince through argumentation. The skeptic invites us, instead, to ask not why we should be committed to any particular belief but why we should believe at all. As Annas explains, the skeptic "regards people who believe things to be good or bad as misguided, and in need of correction; but this is achieved not by altering their beliefs, but by putting them in a position where they can lose them."[66]

The genuinely skeptical alternative, from this point of view, is a suspension of judgment on what are ultimately undecidable differences. The *need to resolve* the difference between right and wrong is the origin of conflict. And since this need is persistent, skepticism can often be confused with subtle forms of dogmatism, like relativism: *the belief* that moral values, for example, are relative.[67] But it may seem that the ancient skeptic is proposing an impossibility. Is it really feasible to live at all without belief? Would there not be a void and complete loss of orientation? Does this not take criticism too far, beyond any reasonable or realistic set of limits? To see why the ancient skeptics' position might be a viable one, it is necessary to consider their understanding of the relationship between nature and culture, an understanding similar to the Nietzschean position outlined above.

It has been stressed that a distinction between nature and culture often guides criticism. The idea that, in comparison with nature, culture is a relative thing capable of change supports the modern critique of ideology. A theorist like Butler goes further in contending that even nature itself is culturally inflected and susceptible to modification. The ancient skeptics, by contrast, adopt the reverse position. They assume nature and culture are continuous with one another and relatively fixed. For the skeptical philosophers, "the handing-down of customs and laws (and the learning of skills) is . . . on a level with the constraints arising from nature as sentient beings with desires (for food, for example) that we can do nothing about."[68] The idea that nature and culture are undifferentiated is usually present *prior* to the introduction of criticism. But, in the view of the ancient skeptics as well as of Nietzsche, it can also arise *after* a period of sustained criticism, once we see there is no possibility of resolving the question about whether our cultural surroundings are right or wrong.[69] As with respect to nature, the very question of the validity of culture then disappears. The suspension of judgment means one is neither committed nor resistant to cultural norms.

This perspective explains why the skeptic is still capable of acting when belief comes to an end. As Annas explains, the skeptic lives a normal life on the outside, meeting obligations and making decisions.[70] From within, however, she thinks and acts without being committed to the goodness or badness, rightness or wrongness of those thoughts and actions. Thought and action are freed from the need for justification. The skeptic acts according to appearances. The categories of morality and value still apply but in a radically different way. "The skeptic has adequate reason for acting in the fact that things appear good or bad to him. And he will have moral intuitions that are the result of his upbringing, so there is no reason to think that he will do wrong because of immediate pressure to do so."[71] Past beliefs still have their effects, things *appear* as right or wrong. But, the loss of commitment to beliefs, the loss of *believing*, means that thought and action take on an altered quality. Rational and emotional commitments come to be seen as no different from bodily and physical movements. They exist and move the skeptic to act in one way or another, but they are not backed up by an inward imperative or prohibition.

Both Nietzsche and the ancient skeptics appear to adopt this paradoxical view of the relationship between nature and culture in their conceptions of criticism. To return to Nietzsche for a moment, while he stresses the importance of freeing oneself from inherited cultural perspectives, this process does not involve *rejecting* such perspectives. It means only gaining distance from them: "I do not refute ideals, I merely draw on gloves in their presence."[72] Education in criticism, therefore, involves:

> Learning to *see*—habituating the eye to repose, to patience, to letting things come to it; learning to defer judgment, to investigate and comprehend the individual case in all its aspects. This is the *first* preliminary schooling in spirituality: *not* to react immediately to a stimulus, but to have the restraining, stock-taking instincts in one's control.[73]

Of course, such an orientation to criticism appears to have quite conservative implications. It seems as though we must lose any standards or grounds for advocating reform and change. Nevertheless, if we are prepared to rethink the way in which desirable reform and change can occur, these reservations might not carry so much weight. As discussed in previous chapters, when criticism is no longer preoccupied with cognitive justification, the theory and practice of cultivation become more important. Then, the origin of social and political reform lies not so much in shared theoretical standards as in work on the level of affective sensibility. Perhaps this could take the form of a cultivation of inward freedom of the Nietzschean and skeptical kind. Such inner freedom may be an important precondition for genuine change since until individuals release themselves from attachment to existing institutions, whether this attachment is of a positive or negative kind, different institutions may be prevented from coming into existence. White makes a similar point when he argues that his "weak ontologists" tend not to call for a wholesale transformation of liberal democracy but suggest instead "different ways of living those structures."[74]

Theorists like Habermas and Butler are resistant to such an approach to criticism and social change. In contrast to the passive, detached, *aesthetic* attitude distinguishing the kind of criticism discussed here, they both emphasize, albeit in different ways, the importance of the "performative" dimension. They conclude that an inward form of *activity* must lead from the destabilization of norms and values. Habermas insists that once we acknowledge the performative dimension, we cannot pretend to treat norms and values as if they are natural artifacts. Rather, we have to take claims to validity "seriously" and avoid "reducing them to something that is simply found in the world."[75] Similarly, Butler argues that "[a]s much as a perspective on the subject requires an evacuation of the first person, a suspension of the 'I' in the interests of an analysis of subject formation, so a reassumption of that first-person perspective is compelled by the question of agency."[76]

In accepting the necessity and desirability of the performative dimension, however, these theorists suppress a different mode of criticism. The general interpretation of western cultural development advanced by Nietzsche offers an explanation of why this need for inward activity and the associated sense of "I-ness" has become compelling. This explanation involves, in general terms, the persistent belief that the world is "for us," that it can be ordered instrumentally and morally according to "humane" ideals.[77] When criticism is guided by this belief, the idea that culture is, in comparison to nature, relative and susceptible to change fits in nicely. Processes of criticism then tend to accentuate the need to act, to resolve or manipulate moral conflicts and oppositions. The sense of being unsettled by critique does not incline toward a passive attitude. In the skeptical form of criticism, by contrast, there is far less emphasis on external change and the need for inward forms of activity to direct such change. Skeptical adventurousness weakens the strength of inward compulsion, allowing individuals to think and act without extraneous burdens of justification and pressures for rationalization. At the same time, skeptical criticism in no way prevents the transformation of cultural forms or institutional structures. On the contrary, it indicates that the cultivation of individuality itself, as a form of freedom and detachment from one's surroundings, is the medium of meaningful change.

The idea of an identity between nature and culture, then, may encourage a shift in the constellation of attitudes and needs often characteristic of modernity. This shift does not mean the cognitive doubts and problems that have preoccupied theorists like Habermas and Butler will disappear. These cognitive issues persist but they appear in a different light. The need for justification driven by the nature/culture divide gives way to a more creative response to such dilemmas and contradictions. The freedom made possible by looking on oneself and others as a spectacle of nature displaces the quest for reassurance with a different attitude toward learning. One becomes more eager to find out about one's place in the natural order of things rather than locate an illusory cultural foundation that is supposed to differentiate us from the rest of nature. One reconceives the challenge posed by questions of belief, becoming less concerned with the validity of belief and more interested in how opinions and convictions are tied up with material processes such as the dynamics of physical embodiment. One embarks on an adventure in nature, without the sense of separateness and alienation of the "I."[78]

These implications of a metaphysic of nature/culture identity are suggestive. While such an ontology establishes important conditions of possibility, there is no guarantee that it will lead to more creative forms of criticism and awareness. Less ambiguous, I believe, are the consequences of efforts to salvage the dimension of performativity. Habermas, in particular, has been relentless in his construction of arguments in defense of the first-person. He insists this is necessary so as to resist the strong pressures toward instrumentalization in the modern world. And yet these pressures, it has been indicated here, are increased precisely by those ontologies that sustain a division between nature and culture. The cultivation of care for and appreciation of the earth will be possible only when we truly see ourselves as part of it.

Part II

Democracy, Aesthetics, and Individuality

4

Habermas's Democratic Proceduralism

If the "foundations" of change and transformation lie in relatively individualized practices of self-cultivation rather than in a secure, shared knowledge, how should we now think about politics? If demands for the world to be otherwise are cognitively ungrounded and insinuate violence, how can merely an increased receptivity to existence serve the requirements of political reform? What place have the aesthetic concerns of individuality in political arenas that require truncated forms of thought and action? Questions like these are raised by the arguments of the first part of this book. "A return to the individual is all well and good," someone may say, "but what has it got to do with the 'real' world of politics where one has to fight and struggle?" "Be careful not to become the monster you are fighting" might be the first part of a response.[1]

This second part of the book examines a selection of the issues arising from the somewhat strained relationships between politics, aesthetics and individuality. It does so by focusing on different strategies for expanding the democratic elements of liberal democracy. This chapter begins the analysis with a consideration of Habermas's account of deliberative democracy. Deliberative understandings of democracy, in general, have been constructed with a particular emphasis on responding to doubts about the feasibility of an extension of democracy beyond its liberal forms. They have sought to provide radical democratic ideals new impetus via a willingness to work with rather than against existing liberal institutions. Deliberative theorists accept that a radically participatory form of democracy is simply impractical in the context of modern society. They seek, therefore, to consider the ways in which participation, discussion, and reasoning can take place within liberal institutions and thereby strengthen their deliberative elements without superseding them. In Bohman's words, "Few deliberative democrats now think of deliberation independently from voting or bargaining. The question is only how to make them more consistent with deliberation rather than undermining it."[2]

This chapter examines deliberative democracy's response to only one of the difficulties facing radical democratization, namely the capacity of the individual to contribute to a more radically democratic organization of social and political life. It is restricted further by focusing on Habermas's theory of deliberative democracy. The chapter begins with an analysis of Habermas's treatment of the question of individual capacity and the role of self-transformation in extending democracy. As discussed in the introduction, theorists like Rorty object to radical democracy because it seems such a project imposes illiberal demands on individuals to become more virtuous. Habermas responds to such doubts by shifting the link between universalism and democracy from the level of individual self-development, where he agrees such a link does have undesirable consequences, to the more abstract level of structures of interaction. The chapter considers, specifically, how this broad approach allows him to locate the basic foundations of democracy at the level of institutional and cultural forms of *proceduralism*. It is argued that Habermas believes procedures act as compensatory devices for personal fallibility and weakness. They make room, in his view, for political participation by individuals at the same time as they ease the burden of responsibility for democracy on individuals as such. The focus on proceduralism is seen to be part of his broader attempt to justify the separation of politics and universal morality from the more concrete concerns of aesthetics and ethics.

Extending the arguments developed in the first part of the book, the chapter then questions the cogency of this deliberative attempt to go beyond liberal democracy. It claims procedural compensations and balances are relatively limited in their effectiveness and, for this reason, democracy is far more dependent on individuals than Habermas would like to admit. The suggestion is put forward, in short, that the aesthetic quality of practices of self-transformation and self-development are central to radical democracy. This argument is developed in two stages. First, it is asserted that Habermas's *cognitive* version of proceduralism jeopardizes the potential of democracy to provide a non-violent mode of conflict resolution. The contention here is that the moral and aesthetic modes of rationality are always interconnected. Habermas's notion that procedures can provide for impartiality by separating the two, therefore, merely heightens the intensity of disagreement among constituencies. It is then argued, second, that the expectations placed by radical democracy on individuals invokes the need for a kind of political theory less anemic than the one provided by Habermas. In particular, theory needs to incorporate aesthetic issues if it is to address questions of motivation given the considerable resources individuals need to divert to deliberation if radical democratic ideals are to be effective in practice.

Procedural Compensations for Weak Individuality

Habermas is critical of pessimistic and fatalistic prognoses that imply that radical democracy has become irrelevant. He believes we should not lose sight of the emancipatory potential of modern society and culture. It is tempting to succumb to a "melancholic mood" of "defeatism" given the tremendous problems and dangers we ourselves have produced and that we are apparently unable to manage via the political process.[3] Such a mood, in Habermas's view, should not exclude a proper analysis of contemporary circumstances. He aims to clarify how the ideals of radical democracy may still be practically realized by offering a "new reading," one that renders these ideals "appropriate to the circumstances of a complex society."[4] Habermas's reinterpretation of radical democracy relies heavily on the notion of *procedure* at a number of different levels. This first section of the chapter sets out the nature and significance of this notion, especially as it aims to compensate for the "weak personality" of modern individuals.

Habermas notes the development of cultural and institutional forms of proceduralism is a modern one. This development has come about because the mechanisms for producing social order and integration have changed. Generally speaking, premodern societies were reproduced through a collective ethos of life. The individual was socialized into a distinct personal identity connected with a specific social role which, in turn, complemented other social roles to form a relatively harmonious system of things. This material background was symmetrical with the structures of metaphysical modes of political philosophy. Such philosophy could, given the stratified organization of society, cultivate a table of universal virtues. It specified principles that rendered individual relationships both ethical in themselves and functional for social stability. This constellation of theory and practice broke down with the onset of modern forms of society and their corresponding structures of thought.[5] The growth of negative freedom and moral uncertainty meant new methods of generating social order were required.

Habermas's articulation of these new methods proceeds via a distinction between the "material" and the "symbolic" aspects of human existence.[6] In the material dimensions of social life, he argues "functional reason" developed to compensate for the dissolution of a tightly controlled politico-economic system. Functional reason operates through "media" of "money" and "power" in the spheres of market and state respectively. It allows for an *integrated* form of self-interested action. The minimum of mutual understanding and regulation required is expressed in the universal rules of media. In the symbolic region of society, a different form of regulation arose as patterns of socialization became less rigid and the plurality of ways of life increased. Here, Habermas claims "procedural reason" provides an abstract unity of concrete differences. Procedures represent a centripetal force in the face of a decreasing fund of value consensus which, among a number of other tendencies, threatens to break up society into a state of conflictual anarchy. It is with Habermas's understanding of procedural reason that this chapter is most concerned.

Habermas asserts the rise of procedural reason, as a central and necessary feature of social integration, explains why radical democratic ideals are built into, and functional for, the modern way of life. Once human beings no longer agree on basic moral norms, he contends, the only thing they share is a belonging to "some communicative form of life." Since these life forms "have certain structural aspects in common," there is a definite foundation on which they are able to coexist.[7] Habermas identifies these common features, in the terms of his theory of communicative action, as structures of "reciprocal recognition" or procedural reason built into ordinary language communication. Procedural reason expresses the essential idea of a democratic form of life, the principle of "impartiality": the idea that the needs and interests of each individual must be taken into account in forming the rules and norms that will regulate their life together.[8] In Habermas's view, democracy takes on a political and institutional existence when individuals mutually accord one another the basic rights and duties required for a discursive and participatory mode of cooperation.[9]

In relation to individual conduct, modern proceduralism performs a double function: it both preserves and compensates for moral uncertainty and moral weakness. Procedures *preserve* moral uncertainty by making clear that questions and issues can never be finally resolved but only continuously addressed through a rational process. This expresses "the radically anti-Platonic insight that there is neither a higher nor a deeper reality to which we c[an] appeal."[10] We must accept our situatedness in this world and orient ourselves only with a reason that is conscious of its fallibility and therefore opens itself up to a cooperative search for answers. A "postmetaphysical" or "postconventional" morality "provides no more than a *procedure* for impartially judging disputed questions. It cannot pick out a catalogue of duties or even designate a list of hierarchically ordered norms, but it expects subjects to form their own judgments."[11] The flipside of this uncertainty, however, is that morality loses the practical foothold in social reality it possessed in premodern contexts: what is right to do is no longer embodied in patterns of cultural life. Individuals are generally confronted with uncertainty about how to act in any given situation. Also, even if knowledge of what to do is available, a morality or rationality that exists only as knowledge implies a degree of moral weakness. An individual must possess a strong will if a principle is to be carried through into action. In modern society, therefore, the task of acting rationally and morally imposes rather onerous demands on the individual who may be repeatedly challenged by a range of sanctions and incentives for acting otherwise. In this respect, Habermas suggests proceduralism plays a *compensatory* role: it "*relieves* the judging and acting person of the considerable cognitive, motivational, and—given the moral division of labor often required to fulfil positive duties—organizational demands of a morality centered on the individual's conscience."[12] Habermas proposes this compensatory process functions at two levels, one legal, the other informal.

Legal Proceduralism

Habermas claims the procedural principles of democracy, with the help of law, take on a considerable degree of practical effectiveness, not only with respect to individual weakness but in relation to social complexity as a whole. This argument about modern law consists of two significant contentions: first, that law plays a crucial role in social integration and, second, that law embodies the structures of reciprocal recognition constitutive of modern proceduralism. With regard to the question of social integration, Habermas believes positive law is the main successor to a concrete cultural ethos in tasks of social integration.[13] He argues the key sociological feature of law is that it "stabilizes behavioral expectations." It lets "members of a social collectivity know what behavior they may demand of one another when and in which situations."[14] Moreover, this stabilizing function is not merely contingent since the legitimacy of law, in Habermas's view, can be traced back to a rational process of democratic opinion- and will-formation. As mentioned above, his discursive concept of democracy involves subjects mutually according one another the basic rights and duties required for rational discourse. The "basic system of rights" that results means citizens are able to view themselves as both the authors and addressees of law.[15] Taken together, these two claims underlay the argument that *legal procedure* is the foundation of a practical and feasible model of deliberative democracy. Law lends potency to a procedural resolution of issues that would otherwise remain dependent on the weak motivations of individuals and confront the morally indifferent dynamics of organizational and bureaucratic force:

> A principled morality whose effectiveness was based solely on socialization processes and individual conscience would remain restricted to a narrow radius of action. Through a legal system with which it remains internally coupled, however, morality can spread to *all* spheres of action.[16]

This procedural account of deliberative democracy indicates why individuals do not shoulder an unbearable proportion of responsibility for democracy. Democratic effectiveness depends, rather, on a collective process that follows along the grooves of a legal procedure. In particular, procedural conditions and rules guarantee a certain quality of public debate and deliberation. Even though debates will always need to be terminated prematurely via some decision-making mechanism such as voting, the outcome can be presumed legitimate for the time being as long as deliberation has followed procedural lines. The resulting law, even while open to further revision, "owes its legitimating force to a *democratic procedure* intended to guarantee a rational treatment of political questions."[17] Individual and group contributions are "forced" through democratic filters "at the social level of institutionalized processes."[18] This understanding makes possible, for Habermas, a model of radical democracy that is independent of its restrictive formulations in some versions of republicanism. Republicanism suggests that both order and democracy depend on the enforcement of an exclusionary range of civic virtues. But with an acknowledgment of how law has extended the scope and power of proceduralist forms, the sense of necessity involved in this equation breaks down.

For Habermas, then, the procedural features of modern law preserve a potential for freedom and autonomy by restraining the functioning of social processes within certain parameters. These procedural parameters keep alive the possibilities of democratic control, as a continuous and ongoing endeavor, even if the conditions for individual autonomy are not completely realized. In this respect, Habermas's approach is similar to Kant's cautious endorsement of democracy. Kant's commitment to modernity as an age of criticism was accompanied by an emphasis on the responsibilities criticism entails. At one place, he makes a distinction between the private and public uses of reason in the interests of allowing individuals the opportunity to become *accustomed* to the exercise of freedom. Thus, while each individual should be allowed complete freedom in their role as "a scholar before the reading public,"[19] enlightenment is done no harm but actually enhanced if freedom of thought is narrowly restricted in one's occupational life:

> Here is shown a strange and unexpected trend in human affairs in which almost everything, looked at in the large, is paradoxical. A greater degree of civil freedom appears advantageous to the freedom of mind of the people, and yet it places inescapable limitations on it; a lower degree of civil freedom, on the contrary, provides the mind with room for each man to extend himself to his full capacity. As nature has uncovered from under this hard shell the seed for which she most tenderly cares—the propensity and vocation to free thinking—this gradually works back on the character of the people, who thereby gradually become capable of managing freedom; finally, it affects the principles of government, which finds it to its advantage to treat men, who are now more than machines, in accordance with their dignity.[20]

Similarly, though with less paternalism, Habermas develops a conception of democracy with an in-built safety mechanism. Procedural law is an acknowledgment that not everyone will take on the collective responsibilities necessary to sustain a condition of freedom:

> To the extent that moral cognition is not sufficiently anchored in the motives and attitudes of its addressees, it must be supplemented by a law that enforces norm-conformative behavior while leaving motives and attitudes open. Coercive law overlays normative expectations with threats of sanctions in such a way that addressees may restrict themselves to the prudential calculation of consequences.[21]

Once again, while premodern identities were infused with potent capacities for moral action, modern ones tend to be overburdened with cognition that is not practically effective. Being more conscious, or more "historical" as Nietzsche remarked, modern culture is also weaker in terms of will and personality.[22] Habermas recognizes this in his Kantian-type approach when he notes that law "can offset the weaknesses of a morality that exists primarily as knowledge."[23] In short, many people may not yet be ready to take on moral responsibilities, especially when moral principles appear so uncertain and moral action is often too risky. Thus, the law, with a certain ideal about self-determination ingrained within it, contains a coercive element that preserves the possibility of further democratization processes by restraining conduct within procedural parameters. It is too dangerous to make society dependent on an autonomous morality, rationality or democracy all at once. Instead, a gradual modification of the capacity of reason to influence insight and will must take place before the law's coercive function can diminish. In the meantime, and perhaps indefinitely, law, through its simultaneously coercive and democratic structure, keeps the doors open for a more active citizenry.

Informal Proceduralism

Habermas's procedural theory of law indicates that, in principle, expectations of individual freedom, social order, and democratic participation are compatible with one another. He admits, though, that this felicitous arrangement can be sustained, in the final instance, only if citizens mobilize their freedom in a responsible way. If individuals pursue merely their own interests under the guise of negative freedom and do not contribute to a civic culture, the coercive aspect of law will be overburdened and democratic possibilities will dry up. Deliberative democracy depends, as one could expect, on the willingness of citizens to deliberate.[24] Even then, however, Habermas argues the burdens on individuals are not as onerous as they may first appear. His conception of procedure extends beyond its formal-legal manifestations to consider how a network of informal-procedural structures provide a further source of relief.

Habermas notes, first, that legal procedures regulate only the formal political system. The strength of law is appropriate to this sphere in which powerful organizations and bureaucracies often seek to subvert procedural restraints. Law is not relevant as a form of regulation in the other domains of social intercourse, particularly in the areas of civil society and the public sphere. Democracy, for Habermas, is rooted ultimately in these domains of human interaction: it has the power to regulate formal spheres only on condition that citizens generate this power through unrestricted practices of opinion-formation. To emphasize the inapplicability of law in informal regions, he describes the public sphere as a "wild," "anarchic" structure that "resists organization as a whole"[25] while civil society is defined as being "nongovernmental," "noneconomic," and "voluntary" in nature.[26]

Habermas argues there is good reason for conceptualizing democracy in terms of a distinction between formal and informal spheres. In the formal realm, the pressure to make decisions means deliberation is inherently distorted, even if it is kept within democratic parameters by legal procedures. In the informal sphere, where such pressures are lessened, deliberation can occur more freely and provide both a stronger epistemic and moral basis to democracy.[27] Compared to the political system, the associations of civil society are more sensitive to social issues and are best suited to developing appropriate interpretations and problem-solutions that can be projected into the public sphere. Also, only in the periphery can there be a progressive struggle over the interpretation of needs and the world as a whole. These interpretations and conceptions usually change over a lengthy period as debate in the public sphere slowly problematizes issues and brings up unquestioned assumptions for explicit discussion. Thus, Habermas proposes a "two-track model" of democracy in which a "constitutionally regulated circulation of power" is maintained only on condition that the "core" political system remains responsive to the "periphery" of the public sphere.[28] This model makes concessions to the logistical requirements of complexity while allowing for cultural change to filter in slowly from a distance: the deeper needs of social coexistence should, over time, work to modify the logics of operation of the engines of state and market.

In these informal domains of deliberation, too, procedures compensate for the variability of individual contributions and the power differentials between groups and individuals. Habermas says there is a "latent dependency built into the internal structure of every public sphere": "the players in the arena owe their influence to the approval of those in the gallery."[29] Since the structures of reciprocal recognition exercise this subtle effect, public debates can be kept within democratic parameters, as long as the political culture is broadly liberal in orientation. Once again, citizens are "relieved" of the exacting expectations of a republican-like virtue. Habermas maintains that while some "orientation to the common good" is necessary, it

> only needs to be exacted in small increments insofar as practical reason withdraws from the hearts and heads of collective or individual actors into the procedures and forms of communication of political opinion- and will-formation. In other words, practical reason shifts from the individual level of ethical motivations and insights to the social level of gathering and processing information.[30]

The upshot is that Habermas hopes to lay to rest an understanding of democracy that relies directly on individual citizens. Given the role procedures play in the legal-formal domain, in the informal areas of civil society and the public sphere, and in the relationship between the two, we can comprehend the conditions of possibility for deliberation without reference to the individual as such. Habermas's efforts here are part of his much broader project of replacing "the philosophy of the subject" with a philosophy of communicative action. This new paradigm is meant to demonstrate that democracy no longer depends on a need to "concentrate sovereignty concretely in the people."

> The "self" of the self-organizing legal community disappears in the subjectless forms of communication that regulate the flow of discursive opinion- and will-formation in such a way that their fallible results enjoy the presumption of being reasonable.[31]

Habermas intimates this "sense" of democracy through the language he uses to describe it. He speaks of "proceduralized popular sovereignty," the "image of a decentered society," a "higher-level intersubjectivity," "subjectless communications," and "flows of communication."[32] Opportunities for democratization arise because procedural structures make possible processes of opinion- and will-formation largely irrespective of the context or the competencies of actors. Habermas cites favorably a passage from an essay by Offe and Preuss, in this regard, which describes how constitutional and democratic institutions "play the role of 'congealed' or 'sedimented' virtue" thus making "the *actual practice* of . . . virtues, such as truthfulness, wisdom, reason, justice and all kinds of exceptional moral qualities, to some extent dispensable—on the part of both the rulers and the ruled."[33]

The Limits of Proceduralism

Habermas makes a persuasive argument about the role of the individual in democracy. No one individual is responsible for democracy because it is a collective practice. The burdens on individuals are not excessively demanding because procedural structures, at both a formal and informal level, provide democratic deliberation with a strength which is almost anonymous. At the same time, though, Habermas seems to concede the individual has an ultimate importance, even if this importance is exaggerated in the republican conceptualization. For, in the final instance, democratic effectiveness depends on the personal capacities of a significant proportion of citizens *as individuals*: each must find the justification and motivation for turning away from purely private concerns and exercising their civic freedoms for the sake of an interest much broader than their own.

> Law can be preserved as legitimate only if enfranchised citizens switch from the role of private legal subjects and take the perspective of participants who are engaged in the process of reaching understanding about the rules for their life in common. To this extent, constitutional democracy depends on the motivations of a population *accustomed* to liberty, motivations that cannot be generated by administrative measures.[34]

Under the modern conditions of negative freedom, this decision to "switch" perspectives is an individual choice. Law allows for a regulated egoism, a "liberation" from communicative obligations.[35] It is an internal condition of democracy that citizens be free *not* to get involved. Negative freedom has a priority since it makes possible genuinely democratic or moral conduct: an imposed democracy or morality would be fictional.

Apathy, however, as a constitutional right, endangers the constitution itself over the course of time. Thus, while the procedural infrastructure of deliberative democracy is crucial as a counterweight to numerous antidemocratic dynamics, procedures lose their democratic spirit without the spirited contributions of individuals. For the reasons examined in chapter 1, Habermas refuses to systematically incorporate the theme of individuality in a way that might address the problem of apathy. Once again, it can be seen how his approach draws on functionalist considerations in an attempt to respond to the issues. Along functionalist lines, then, Habermas suggests that a subtle dynamic works against apathy and almost compels individuals to engage in democratic discourse. For him, citizens are necessarily motivated, whether consciously or unconsciously, to pursue collective goals and regulate their conflicts with one another *consensually*. Even as traditional, substantive agreements are eroded, an insistent need remains for individuals to live together cooperatively. And even if agreement is unlikely, the one thing that still rationally motivates every participant to *keep trying* to resolve his or her conflicts consensually is the legal and democratic assurance that their needs and interests will be recognized, that issues will be resolved impartially.

In Habermas's view, if the proceduralism of democracy did not have its roots in the communicative structure of life, it would not be distinguishable from violent or strategic approaches to dealing with problems. The presuppositions of discourse preserve the distinction between myth and enlightenment and enable a process of democratic learning. When we act, Habermas argues, we necessarily bring along a claim to validity: we claim the action has a validity in relation to universal standards that transcend time and place. These "idealizing" presuppositions create a "tension between facticity and validity." While every claim is addressed to a particular audience at a particular time and place, it simultaneously "refers to the ideally expanded audience of the unlimited interpretation community that would have to be convinced for the speech act to be justified and, hence, rationally acceptable."[36] We are, for this reason, propelled into a dynamic and cooperative learning process, a search for the truth about things. We may accept the validity of claims for the time being, but only as one stop along a potentially endless process of contestation and revision that leads toward enlightenment. Habermas maintains we actually have "no choice," since we are "forced" to deal with political problems with reference to procedural standards of impartiality.[37] As mentioned in chapter 3, while this may be "dogmatism," in his view it is "harmless."[38]

At this point in the argument, then, Habermas pulls out his trump card, drawing on the significant theoretical resources of the theory of communicative action. However, this move simultaneously exposes a notable weakness in his reasoning about democracy. This weakness concerns his method of justifying the procedural principles of deliberation. In this respect, Habermas has been charged, even by friendly critics, with prescribing overly demanding requirements for democracy, requirements that actually jeopardize rather than enable its capacity to provide an alternative to the potential violence contained in pluralism and diversity.[39] It may seem that Habermas's procedural and discursive concept of democracy is not overly exacting for citizens since it relies on no prior, substantive consensus. It depends only on commitment to the principle of impartiality, or what he calls (D). But given the divergent outlooks and life experiences of individuals and groups in modernity, citizens may not be able to agree on what impartiality involves. Each group may see the other's definition of impartiality as inimical to their interests. Habermas's claim that impartiality is a shared, universal principle is designed to rise above these sectarian points of view. Thomas McCarthy argues, to the contrary, that "[t]he separation of formal procedure from substantive content is never absolute: we cannot agree on what is just without achieving some measure of agreement on what is good."[40] From this perspective, formal principles have no definite meaning in and of themselves but are interpreted in light of broader conceptions of life as a whole. Social life is characterized as a struggle for meaning within which divergent conceptions of justice first find their place. By pitching the minimum requirements of democracy at too high a level, it is implied, Habermas risks reintroducing the destructive elements of modernity he is trying to set aside.[41]

The concepts of consensus and impartiality are, nonetheless, crucial in Habermas's account. Citizens need to distinguish impartially between what he calls the "moral," "ethical" and "pragmatic" aspects of political problems in order to embark on appropriate types of discourse and bargaining.[42] Still, if they cannot overcome reasonable disagreements at this preliminary stage, then discursive democracy must fail in practical terms. Instead of "spurring on"[43] democratic processes, critics suggest the motivation for consensus may well produce disappointment and disaffection. The implication is that the legitimacy of democracy may derive from its superior ability to resolve problems that *do not* admit of consensus. Habermas's identification of the willingness of citizens to resolve conflicts nonviolently with the motivation for consensus would then be misplaced. It would amount to a strenuous insistence on rationality to the detriment of practicality, even of the very reasonableness that is supposed to ensue from giving up on the universal status of particular ethical perspectives.

Perhaps the stark contrast between consensus- and strategically oriented action needs to be given way if Habermas is to accommodate these points. Then, even on explicitly moral questions, discourse would have to make room for elements of bargaining and fair compromise if democracy is to be workable. In general, the "normative account of legitimacy" would need to be broadened "to recognize forms of compromise that are not simply based on strategic calculations."[44] The question of whether such concessions to strategic action necessarily amount to a downgrading of the normative content of democracy would then depend on the quality of the political culture. It has already been noted that Habermas does not underestimate the significance of practices of both a formal and informal kind. He insists that "any universalistic morality is dependent on a form of life that *meets it halfway*. There has to be a modicum of congruence between morality and the practices of socialization and education. . . . Moral universalism is a *historical result*."[45] But critics suggest this does not remedy the problem since Habermas's reconstruction of culture is itself too rationalistic. McCarthy points out a different way of relying on a "form of life."[46] He argues it is possible to imagine situations in which participants may still be *motivated* to engage in debate through the idea of consensus, rather than merely seek a compromise of interests, *even though they may regard the actual achievement of consensus to be unrealistic*. This would not mean, as it does for Habermas, that the very grammar of our existence would break down, that the idea of truth would lose all credibility and orienting force. Rather, there could be a type of community that cultivated "good-willed members" to keep on searching for the common interest.[47] Consistent with the arguments presented throughout this book, a relaxation of cognitive requirements might give way to a different orientation to knowledge and interaction. Individuals could cultivate sensibilities and dispositions suited to a vibrant and sensitive form of democracy, in other words, by first being freed from functional pressures toward consensus.[48]

In light of these considerations, it becomes clear that Habermas's theory of deliberative democracy attempts, in fact, a double movement away from the individual. In the first part of the chapter, one dimension of this retreat from citizens was examined, in terms of a "spatial" relocation of democratic foundations. Insofar as his theory still has implications for the individual, however, these implications relate only to certain aspects of the individual. Mark Warren emphasizes this point in a reconstruction of Habermas's approach that highlights the role of the self in discursive democracy.[49] Warren underlines a number of ways in which Habermas contributes to an understanding of the potential for, and nature of, self-transformation in processes of radical democratization.[50] He also notes, nevertheless, along with other critics, that Habermas tends to work with and assume only a thin, cognitive and linguistic theory of the self. Such a theory of the self appears to conceptualize adequately the individual traits required for democratic deliberation, in particular the need for orientation to standards such as consensus and impartiality. But it does so only at the cost of excluding and even repressing other dimensions of the self. More important, Habermas seems to ignore the deeper emotional and affective elements of subjectivity which may be critical for both an individual's decision to enter public debates and their manner of contributing. To be fair, Warren acknowledges such criticisms do not quite hit their target since they ignore the motivations of Habermas's work:

> Unlike Freud, Habermas does not start with the demands of the self against society, but rather with *political* problems. The importance of Habermas's initial problematic cannot be overemphasized. His question is: What must we demand of the self *if* we wish our political life to be governed by talk rather than coercion, autonomous structures, or blind consensus? It is from this perspective that Habermas reaches into the self, but it is *only a reaching*, only an interest in those competencies that might best fit the demands of the self with the demands of political life, which we have no a priori way of knowing to be the same.[51]

Even from a political perspective, though, it may be argued that the deeper elements of the self are still very relevant.[52] In the next and final part of the chapter, there is a more detailed consideration of the relevance of individuality in order to further emphasize the significance of aesthetic issues to the politics of democracy.

Expectations of Individuals in Radical Democracy

Habermas admits that the effectiveness of deliberation depends on more than just procedures. Deliberation works well only insofar as "the problems at hand are sensitively perceived, adequately described, and productively answered in the light of a reflexive, posttraditional transmission of culture."

> Reaching mutual understanding through discourse indeed guarantees that issues, reasons, and information are handled reasonably, but such understanding still depends on contexts characterized by a capacity for learning, both at the cultural and the personal level. In this respect, dogmatic worldviews and rigid patterns of socialization can block a discursive mode of sociation.[53]

Habermas suggests, then, that sensibilities, dispositions and attitudes play an integral role in discourse. Other elements of his theoretical work add support to this observation and grate against his line of reasoning about proceduralism. Of particular significance is his articulation of the relationship between "validity claims" and "identity claims." As discussed in chapter 1, Habermas's theory of communicative action develops an understanding of the self as constitutively dependent on interactive relationships. This helps explain why modern identity is notoriously weak and unstable. Individuals are no longer prescribed identities from birth in the way characteristic of premodern societies, but required to establish an identity in processes of interaction. In this respect, Habermas highlights the ambivalence of modernization processes by referring to them as instances of "release and isolation."[54] The freedom gained through release simultaneously means isolation from a stable symbolic framework. Intersubjective dependencies are accentuated in modernity as individuals come to rely further on the qualities of interaction for their sense of identity. We are exposed to a precarious existence, he says, not so much in terms of "cruder threats to the integrity of life and limb," but in an "almost constitutional insecurity and chronic fragility of personal identity."[55] This fragility makes democracy a potentially hazardous affair. If already feeling threatened and insecure, subjects may have difficulty disassociating discussions about issues from discussions about themselves and the "potential for irritability grows."[56] Their understanding of the world is then shaped by a narcissistic quality so that encounters with others become a test of self-worth. Communicative action is precluded by either a manifest or latent pursuit of self-defense or self-aggrandizement.[57]

Insofar as history is also progress, argues Habermas, it can be understood as an extrication of "validity" from "identity." The two tend to be intertwined in a specific way in less rational ways of life: one's identity is dependent on subscription to particular views. There is little sense of one's own self in distinction from fixed understandings of the world. When this fusion of validity and identity is overcome, the structural potentialities of language are released. It becomes possible for individuals to develop an abstract sense of identity or responsibility through the very process of testing the various validity claims attached to their knowledge. Indeed, identity can be detached from validity only once the domain of validity itself has been internally differentiated. As noted in the introduction, only with the differentiation of the cognitive, moral and aesthetic do worldviews become susceptible to criticism.[58] This is the historical context, then, of the Habermasian concept of democracy. As our shared understandings of the world are eroded, we come to rely more and more on formal identity structures. Autonomy (identity) and rationality (validity) become related to one another in a distinctive way at the modern stage of evolution: the stabilization of abstract identity depends more and more on discourses in which validity claims are differentiated from one another and thematized on their own terms.

Habermas recognizes a significant danger in the process of historical evolution in which an abstract sense of identity is gradually separated from claims to validity: "The revenge of a culture exploited over millennia for the legitimation of domination [might] take this form: Right at the moment of overcoming age-old repressions, it would harbor no violence but it would have no content either."[59] He acknowledges, in other words, that a cultural tradition whose prejudices have been so thoroughly criticized may leave only abstract identity structures behind. Yet, it was just those cultural interpretations of the world which gave human life its meaning. There is the possibility that autonomy may be realized to end up supporting a process of criticism that has lost its object. The relentless erosion of substantive worldviews places increased pressure on structures of reciprocal recognition to take the load of keeping society together. But even if this succeeds, life might thereby become meaningless—there may be nothing left to talk about or fight for.

In practice, of course, this tendency toward nihilism does not necessarily bring a rationalistic dystopia in which human beings become numb and lifeless. The siphoning off of validity often means, instead, vigorous and desperate struggles to reenchant the world. For Habermas, this is the specter of "dedifferentiation." Democracy is put at risk by these struggles insofar as identities are reassured only via a linkage with dogmatic claims to validity. It is precisely for this reason that Habermas refuses to lower the normative requirements of democracy by *weakening* the epistemic justification of discourse. He insists that abstract identity structures represent a democratic threshold and only an orientation toward rational consensus can keep violence at bay. But as has been argued, an insistence on such demanding requirements for democracy may be equally threatening and contain their own, ample potentials for violence. Moreover, this cognitive, rationalistic bias prevents Habermas from considering different ways of "meeting individuals halfway" in the request for more deliberative orientations. Such a critique of Habermas was alluded to in chapter 1 and now I would like to elaborate on its elements further by focusing on questions to do with the *motivations* for being democratic.

If abstract identity structures are not sufficient, on their own, to support exacting deliberative processes, then I would contend that theory needs to reconstruct additional conditions of possibility of radical democracy. Here, we are concerned with the scope for theory to address questions of individual motivation. The issues involved can be initially considered in relation to moral thought and behavior. Questions of morality might be divided into three aspects: the "what," the "how," and the "why." In general, the "what" refers to the rules and principles of morality, while the "how" and "why" involve all those considerations relevant to a human organism developing a sensibility and willingness to think and act in ways consistent with the "what" of morality.[60] As noted above, it is typical in modernity for a certain stage of moral competence not to be matched by an emotional and affective capacity to employ this competence in the stress of open conflict. Habermas acknowledges that such motivational problems encountered in acting morally are not simply a question of morality itself but an issue of the way one experiences life as a whole. And yet he systematically restricts himself to addressing questions to do with the "what" of morality. In this respect, he is the first to admit that his theory does not examine everything there is to know about morality. Habermas aims to clarify what he calls "the moral point of view," which is the cognitive orientation speakers and hearers need to adopt if they are to resolve practical questions in a way consistent with morality. He simply admits that he cannot answer questions of motivation, such as "Why be moral?" or "Why be democratic?" for people themselves. Philosophers, according to him, can provide only theoretical arguments for why morality, rationality, or democracy are crucial for human coexistence in modern societies. For some people this may, itself, be some kind of motivation. Even for them, nonetheless, it is a weak source. Moral despair or moral indifference cannot be overcome with theories. They require "an answer to the fundamental ethical question of the meaning of life as such, of personal or collective identity." Philosophy is unsuited to this "propaedeutic task" in Habermas's view. It

> is not in a privileged position when it competes with the rhetorically moving, exemplary representations of the novelist or the quietly insistent intuitions of common sense. We learn what moral, and in particular immoral, action involves *prior* to all philosophizing. . . . The inarticulate, socially integrating experiences of considerateness, solidarity, and fairness shape our intuitions and provide us with better instruction about morality than arguments ever could.[61]

The key point, for Habermas, is that existential concerns cannot be answered in a universal way in modernity. Such concerns and problems admit only of particular resolutions. Modern philosophy and social theory reflect on a disenchanted world in which a differentiated reason can be unified only in an abstract, formal, and procedural way. This kind of theory simply offers no consolation or support in the face of the "basic risks of existence (guilt, sickness, death)."[62] The only level of life susceptible to reflection by social and political theory is, therefore, made up of the general collective structures of society. It is a desirable development that "solutions" to existential questions are no longer *imposed* on individuals by a tightly integrated social structure in which cognitive, moral, and aesthetic values are neatly interconnected. But surely these questions are still urgent. And should they not be addressed by philosophers such as Habermas? Is it enough to just leave individuals alone to decide for themselves about deeper philosophical questions, and whether or not they would like to participate in deliberative processes?

As we have seen, Habermas concedes that democracy is made up of much more than procedures but as philosophers and social theorists, he maintains that we are not allowed to talk about these additional factors. We should not, in other words, talk about the "why" and "how" of either morality or democracy. However, is it not rather academic to spend so much time trying to justify the moral and democratic points of view when the most pressing questions involve understanding *how* individuals can act in ways more consistent with morality and democracy as well as *why* they should do so? As Bennett notes, "a large quantity of energy [has] to be present in order to make finite selves spend some of their limited resources, to make them give away something of themselves to other beings."[63] And yet the focus on cognitive justification contributes very little to an understanding about how this energy can be brought about.

William Connolly observes that since Habermas "appears to think that because no organization of public life can *resolve* or *eliminate* existential suffering, these issues can be excluded from public discourse."[64] As suggested above, Habermas believes theory can only offer an understanding of how collectively imposed but *extraneous* social burdens can be minimized, burdens that make the *inevitable* risks of life much more difficult to manage than they need be. Connolly acknowledges, along with Habermas, that there are indeed good reasons for making this kind of distinction between, on the one hand, socially and politically induced suffering and, on the other hand, unavoidable existential suffering.[65] Habermas's separation of the moral and political from the aesthetic and ethical is elaborated with this distinction between forms of suffering in mind. Connolly argues, nonetheless, that we cannot compartmentalize our engagement with these two dimensions of suffering in the way Habermas would like. Habermas fails to acknowledge, in Connolly's view, that

> how people come to terms privately and publicly with existential issues bears a profound relation to how they engage the issue of identity, and that how they define the question of individual and associational identity bears a similarly close relation to the way collective identity is lived. Habermas is tempted by the wish to exclude existential issues from political theory, but, again, they seep back in.[66]

In other words, the efficacy of democracy is too dependent on the inner life of the individual to leave out existential and metaphysical issues. Questions about the "how" and "why" of living as a whole infiltrate democratic discourse, just as democratic structures regulate the way in which individuals cope with the inherent pressures of life.

There is a strong argument, then, against Habermas's attempt to shift the foundations of radical democracy from individuals to procedures. As indicated in chapter 1, on seeing that linguistic structures dissolve into the embodied lives of individuals, critical theory needs to be reoriented in a social psychological and even physiological direction in order to better appreciate the role of personality structures in the dynamics of politics. Still, the question arises whether democratic theory and democracy itself can be extended in this way without falling into the dangers theorists such as Habermas, as well as Rorty, are so keen to avoid. Can democratic theory and practice attend to existential concerns in a manner consistent with the freedom and autonomy of individuals in a liberal society? Constructive responses to this challenging question are considered in the next chapter.

5

Democracy and Individuality

Kateb and Connolly

This chapter considers what is loosely termed an "existential" appreciation of the role of the individual in efforts to further democratize liberal societies. It focuses on the contemporary reception of the writings of Emerson and Nietzsche in the work of George Kateb and William Connolly respectively. Kateb and Connolly, it is argued, provide an alternative way of going beyond narrow liberal restrictions on democracy in comparison to Habermas. They do not respond to Rorty's objections about the supposedly illiberal effects of radicalizing democracy by heading off into a theory of proceduralism. Rather, they remain at a more individualized level of analysis and aim to break the link that frightens both Habermas and Rorty, the link between self-transformation and philosophical universalism. In their existential approach, the skepticism characteristic of democracy is itself seen to be the impetus behind individual self-development. The claim in this chapter is that this theoretical scheme is superior to the deliberative understanding of how the democratic dimensions of liberalism can be enhanced. The existential approach recognizes the significance of the individual and it gives aesthetic concerns a central place.

There is, however, a line of reasoning in this chapter which problematizes the relationship between democracy and individuality. From the point of view of democratic effectiveness, practices of self-cultivation in which aesthetic qualities are emphasized may well be essential. But from the perspective of individuals qua individuals, democratic participation may not be an important value or priority in efforts to develop a more aesthetic appreciation of the world. This potential contradiction between democracy and individuality is evident to various degrees and in different ways in the work of the thinkers discussed here. There are tensions, in other words, between the aesthetic qualities of individual self-development and the political drive toward democratic participation. Democracy and the individual seem to be both mutually interdependent and at odds with one another.

The writings of Kateb and Connolly are probed with these apparent contradictions and tensions in mind. The first section of the chapter sets out briefly the "existential" background of these thinkers by considering common aspects of the philosophies of Emerson and Nietzsche. The second section examines Kateb's concept of "democratic individuality" while the third section analyses Connolly's ideas about "arts of the self" and their role in political interaction. Kateb and Connolly diverge in their understanding of the place political participation can and should play in the lives of modern individuals. Generally speaking, Kateb believes there is already significant space for individuality in modern culture, while Connolly insists on the importance of political struggle as a precondition for creating such space. Reflection on these differences in viewpoint will serve as a prelude to the more definitive conclusions reached in the next and final chapter, conclusions about the appropriate relations between politics, aesthetics, and individuality.

Democracy and the Existential Dimension

The exclusion of existential and metaphysical themes from political philosophy is motivated by a belief that no universal and incontestable knowledge of such themes is now possible. Theorists such as Habermas and Rorty agree on this point. They differ, according to Rorty, only when Habermas seeks universalism at the level of democratic procedure: "As far as I can see, one can go along with Habermas up to the point at which he opts for universalism, and then swerve off."[1] But both definitely rule out the possibility of a kind of universality at the existential level. They fail to consider this possibility, I think, because each connects questions of individual identity with substantive, metaphysical knowledge *along cognitive lines*. Identity, for Habermas, is about knowledge of the good life that can only be particular, while Rorty argues the resolution of existential dilemmas requires the cognitive specification of the nature of human beings.[2] In my view, though, the proceduralism both endorse at the public level, as an appropriate medium of individual interaction, can be extended into identity itself. With this extension, understanding identity means not so much focusing on its objective grounding in substantive knowledge, than with the *ways* and *means* individuals relate to such knowledge. To have ontological and metaphysical conceptions is a transcendental necessity, but one's relationship with these conceptions is open to the work of aesthetic cultivation.

Rorty develops a few thoughts in this direction himself, without carrying them through, when he observes the moral dimension of a skeptical and aesthetic-playful method of relating to knowledge. In reassuring his readers about the relativistic approach he adopts towards traditional philosophical questions, he says he would like to

> make one point to offset the air of light-minded aestheticism. . . . This is that there is a moral purpose behind this light-mindedness. The encouragement of light-mindedness about traditional philosophical topics serves the same purposes as does the encouragement of light-mindedness about traditional theological topics. . . . Moral commitment, after all, does not require taking seriously all the matters that are, for moral reasons, taken seriously by one's fellow citizens. It may require just the opposite. It may require trying to josh them out of the habit of taking those topics so seriously. There may be serious reasons for so joshing them. More generally, we should not assume that the aesthetic is always the enemy of the moral.[3]

From this point of view, skepticism can be a positive, moral force which may even lead, although Rorty would not like to go this far, to the kind of self-transformation required for radical democratic practice. Often, though, skepticism is thought merely to result in the impotence of philosophy, in its inability to offer a universal point of view on anything but the most formal and abstract questions. To be sure, Habermas and Rorty emphasize the positive, collective role of skepticism: it makes room for democracy in society as a whole. But they both conclude skepticism undermines the public, philosophical treatment of the existential issues facing individuals.

Ralph Waldo Emerson and Friedrich Nietzsche, on the other hand, provide examples of mobilizing a skeptical, playful, and experimental approach to knowledge and philosophy as the most appropriate way to think through the requirements of individuality. Both emphasize how the individual's relationship to knowledge affects their vitality, energy, or power and thus their capacity to live well amid the contingencies of human existence. Emerson, for instance, argues that the need for cognitive certainty destroys self-reliance. Such need forms part of that tendency to lose trust in ourselves, look outward and become like others for the sake of security. It makes "society" possible, "a joint-stock company, in which the members agree, for the better securing of his bread to each shareholder, to surrender the liberty and culture of the eater." Here, the "virtue in most request is conformity. Self-reliance is its aversion."[4] In a condition of fear and uncertainty, individuals find reassurance in "belonging" with others by subscribing to shared beliefs and outlooks. This conformity, however, is no real anchor and because fears and hopes are tied to external circumstances, the individual suffers from a permanent anxiety that drains them of energy: the "vast majority" are "victims of gravity, custom, and fear."[5] What is needed is the strength to question and enquire, to doubt the entire network of influences in which one is caught up, to "not be hindered by the name of goodness, but . . . explore if it be goodness."[6]

In order to build a foundation within oneself, Emerson believes it is necessary to minimize one's vulnerability in a world of contradictory forces and stormy change. He advises the need for a wise, practical skepticism. This involves resisting prejudice, dogma and even the alluring charm of morality and virtue. It is a "self-containing,"[7] not pretending to know more than one knows, or affecting to be more than one is. Affirmation or denial, in this light, means a premature commitment and partisanship, a sacrifice of one's doubts and of one's openness to the present reality. Individual independence and freedom require detachment from these ordinary human temptations of identification. Emerson suggests the skeptical approach preserves energy for the endless challenges posed by one's environment:

> We cannot give ourselves too many advantages in this unequal conflict, with powers so vast and unweariable ranged on one side, and this little conceited vulnerable popinjay that a man is, bobbing up and down into every danger, on the other. It is a position taken up for better defense, as of more safety, and one that can be maintained; and it is one of more opportunity and range: as, when we build a house, the rule is to set it not too high nor too low, under the wind, but out of the dirt.[8]

In the case of Nietzsche, we have already considered his view of the diverse aftereffects of knowledge in modernity in chapter 3. He emphasizes, in general, the differences between dogmatism and skepticism, between resentment and cheerfulness in thinking about how one can come to terms with doubt and uncertainty. Like Emerson, he claims skepticism and cheerfulness short-circuit an emotional and energy-sapping approach to life. For Nietzsche, "learning to defer judgment" is particularly important if one is to avoid becoming mere fodder for one of the numerous herdlike masses that constitute society. "All unspirituality, all vulgarity," he says, "is due to the incapacity to resist a stimulus—one *has* to react, one obeys every impulse. In many instances, such a compulsion is already morbidity, decline, a symptom of exhaustion."[9] To revitalize oneself, to gain the power to stand alone means building up one's tolerance for the solitary heights and learning to live in the "ice and high mountains"[10] of skepticism.

The formulations of individual autonomy to be found in Emerson and Nietzsche, nevertheless, are not necessarily consistent with a commitment to democratic participation. Indeed, many of their arguments imply a profound contradiction between these two ideals. The cultivation of individuality, for them, tends to be a private affair, too subtle and delicate to be introduced into the brutal dynamics of public interaction in democratic societies. For both thinkers, the proper relationship between politics and culture is one in which the former serves the needs of the latter. To become cultured, they believe, individuals must be free to live contemplatively, undistracted by the demands of utilitarian values. In modern society, however, culture is tailored to the lust for power and prestige embodied in politics and the state. The spaces for individual self-culture are compressed as political, military, and economic achievements become the guiding lights of human endeavor.[11] Moreover, democracy, in their view, can only accelerate these developments as the mass begins to pursue advantages through political means. Nietzsche claims democracy crowds out all that is unequal and different as "the grumbling, oppressed, rebellious slave classes . . . aspire after domination—they call it 'freedom.'"[12] Emerson links democracy with cultural decline in a discussion where he says "the form of government which prevails, is the expression of what cultivation exists in the population which permits it."[13] As Stack remarks, these theorists believe there should be a reduction rather than expansion in the scope of the political realm, but this will only be possible with a growth in individuality, with "a revolution in thought, sensibility, feeling, attitude, and values, a revolution in culture."[14]

For contemporary thinkers who emphasize the importance of individuality to democracy, important questions are raised by the reflections of Emerson and Nietzsche. For example, while a radicalization of liberal democracy may require a basis in strong individuality, does the cultivation of strong individuality not encourage an abandonment of the worldly and collective aspirations of democratic self-determination? From the perspective of the individual, in particular, is political and democratic participation necessary for, or inimical to, a project of self-transformation? Such questions as these are especially pertinent to the work of George Kateb and William Connolly since they appropriate elements of Emerson and Nietzsche respectively in their reflections on democracy. In the remaining parts of this chapter, I would like to explore the writings of these contemporary theorists so as to consider the affinities and tensions between democracy and the individual, and between the political and the aesthetic more broadly. For even if their work provides a way around the dilemmas of strengthening the individualist elements of liberal democracy posed by the likes of Habermas and Rorty, there are other, related problems with their theories that need to be examined.

Kateb and Emerson: Tensions Between the Moral and the Aesthetic

In George Kateb's view, just as Nietzsche sought to think through the implications of the "death of God," the "Emersonians" reflected on what is involved in living with a consciousness of the relativity of social and moral convention.

The Emersonians—Emerson, Thoreau, Whitman—believed individuality becomes possible with the development of such a consciousness. Their aim was to encourage individuality, "to liberate human energies; they all call their readers to live more intensely" now the pressures of conformity from tradition and religion have weakened.[15] In the context of a young America, nonetheless, their promotion of individuality took on a specifically democratic color, since American democracy, for Kateb, was the first and still the best expression of the principles of individualism. In contrast to the theorizations of individuality to be found in other traditions, Kateb sees the Emersonians as initiating a unique and rich body of thought that revolves around what he calls "democratic individuality."

> Their work is suffused by the sense that the political arrangements of democracy conduce to a people's ability to glimpse—if only hesitantly or occasionally—the merely conventional nature of conventions, of most rules and most laws. All pay tribute to the American political system, despite their continuous guardedness. . . . Democracy unsettles everything (though not all at once) and therefore permits the slow growth of individuality. But it unsettles everything for everyone, and thus liberates *democratic* individuality.[16]

The democratic political process, from this point of view, has a broad, cultural function: it creates the space in which individualism can flourish. In comparison to other political systems in which individuals are systematically excluded, ignored, and made to suffer for "higher" political, collective, and "aesthetic" goals, constitutional democracies inculcate a quite different effect. Partisan dispute, procedural constraints, and the discipline of elections, in particular, mold a democratic rather than authoritarian culture in which individual human dignity is the normative standard.

> The perspective of rights-based individualism is suspicious of the political realm. Yet . . . the manner in which constitutional democratic government is put together and does its business radiates powerful moral and existential lessons that help to engender a distinctive culture. . . . The cardinal fact is that the form and routine political and legal workings of constitutional democracy give reality to personal and political rights. In doing so, the system impresses the meaning of rights on the psyche; behavior is changed because everyone's self-conception is changed.[17]

While many individuals will be prepared to play the political game, the game's real benefit is not for them insofar as their egoistic interests are concerned. Rather, its effect is to create a broader cultural framework in which everyone is given the opportunity of cultivating their individuality. "The democratic political game calls for some individuals to lend their less-than-best selves to activity whose meaning is not confined to itself but spreads outward to benefit all individuals."[18]

Kateb may seem to be your average liberal democrat, someone who focuses much more on rights and much less on the collective preconditions of existence. Certainly, he believes "respect for individual rights is the best way of honoring human dignity, by which I mean the equal dignity of every individual."[19] And unlike Rawls who aims to justify *why* individual rights are most important, Kateb simply chooses "to start inside a mode of thinking in which individuals and their rights are assumed as primary because all competing matters urged as primary can be seen as lesser, even when not fictional or unreal."[20] He is, then, a political minimalist who is biased against the state and group politics even while he recognizes the debt individuality owes to constitutional government. Kateb is not a radical democrat, but he is critical of the possessive and complacent forms of individualism widespread in modern democracies. As we shall see, these modes of individualism actually represent, for him, types of groupism that are inimical to genuine individuality. Kateb believes that an individuality requiring hard work and the continuous practice of self-cultivation is necessary to sustain and strengthen democratic culture rather than direct forms of political participation.

Kateb draws heavily on Emerson's notion of self-reliance to develop the concept of democratic individuality, since he believes Emerson is the first and best theorist of the kind of self required for a radically democratic culture.[21] Emerson's life and work illustrate how such a demanding idea of individuality is in tension with the political aspects of democracy, even while those aspects provide support for individuality. The contradictions involve, in part, a conflict between the *aesthetic* qualities of individuality and the *moral* dimensions of democratic political institutions. Kateb reflects on the issues thrown up by this conflict, at one point, by drawing out a distinction between two kinds of self-reliance to be found in Emerson's writings, "mental self-reliance" and "active self-reliance." I will begin by reviewing the relationship between these forms of self-reliance before considering the broader tension articulated by Kateb between democracy and the individual.

Mental self-reliance involves withdrawing one's attachments and commitments to ideas and ways of seeing the world. This does not mean a mental void, rather an ability to enter and exit a variety of perspectives, each with its own distinctive perceptions and sensations. It is particularly important to self-reliance, in this reading of Emerson, that one is able to be impartial in relation to contradictory worldviews. Kateb describes mental self-reliance as "the readiness to treat with sympathetic understanding ideas and values that have no sympathy for one another. In order to develop such understanding, one must try to remain not free of substantive commitments, but sparing of them."[22] It is, therefore, an open-minded perspectivism, an "intellectual method," in which the imagination resists being captured by one specific habit of interpretation. Such a mode of philosophical conduct allows the individual to remain receptive to the contingency and ambiguity of the world. It avoids a dull, routine mental life in which thought follows a pattern of attraction and repulsion dictated by a rigid and narrow economy of likes and dislikes. Kateb argues this kind of individuality is essential for a society aspiring toward democracy since such a "democracy of intellect" is just as important as the external manifestations of democracy.[23] This is especially so over the course of time when democratic institutions and structures themselves form a tradition on which it is tempting to rest, relieved of the rigors of inward independence.

Nevertheless, mental self-reliance is difficult given that desires for certainty and commitment tend to be strong. Kateb suggests it is a process requiring persistent struggle rather than being a stable condition. Since it is easy for individuals to "slide into the vacant places of the last generation,"[24] the intellectual spirit of democracy survives only with constant attention and vigilance. This demand is onerous enough, but Kateb adds to the sense of strenuousness when he discusses the idea of active self-reliance. Human existence manifests not only at the level of the mind but in the dimension of action, both physical and symbolic. Independence and autonomy in these spheres are also important to democratic individuality. Self-reliance faces acute adversities, however, in the practical realm. To begin, there is an apparently innate obstacle working against the expression of inner powers in worldly activity: the individual's lack of consistency. "A man acts not from one motive," says Emerson, "but from many shifting fears and short motives; it is as if he were ten or twenty less men than himself, acting at discord with one another, so that the result of most lives is zero."[25] Even if there is consistency, the individual also faces an outside world that offers a restrictive range of limited opportunities for self-realization. The simple pressures of action in everyday life add to these problems and indicate both the relative ease and intrinsic superiority of contemplative modes of freedom.

Kateb's particular interest in the relation between mental and active self-reliance concerns a direct tension between them regarding the issue of political commitment. Is self-reliance, he asks, compatible with political commitment? This is an urgent question, for Kateb, because of a growing need to practically combat the evil in the world. Given the tremendous degree of unnecessarily inflicted suffering on planet earth, it seems obligatory for individuals to commit themselves to addressing and minimizing this suffering. And yet such practical activity, and the various political exigencies and expediencies it brings with it, contradicts the spirit of detachment involved in the ideal of democratic individuality. Kateb emphasizes, at this point, the *aesthetic* quality of mental self-reliance: self-reliance allows and encourages one to view a contradictory world as a beautiful scene, as possessing a sense of innocence even in its violence. Nevertheless, if the evils are so great, must morality not displace such an aesthetic attitude for the sake of decency and a good conscience?

> I would suggest that the great obstacle to finding self-reliance a genuine ideal is the chance that innocence is no longer possible, no longer defensible. . . . In Emerson's time, one could affirm inexhaustible life despite suffering and wrongdoing with some plausible hope that one was not a coward or a cruel aesthete. But in this century, is this hope tolerable?[26]

Kateb refers to Emerson's own difficulties in choosing between his cherished ideal of self-reliance and a commitment to the collective fight against slavery. In deciding to be committed, Emerson was required to modify his views on political reform which he tended to devalue in relation to individual self-reform. Emerson, in Kateb's view, had to break his sacred promise to self-reliant values for the sake of solidarity in the face of the absolute and unconditional evil of slavery. Emerson's sympathetic understanding, on this issue, reached its limit: "The case is so bad, that all the right is on one side."[27] The ideal of self-reliance is put to one side, here, for the sake of an organized, non-individualistic struggle.

Contemporary circumstances, for Kateb, have made things much harder for us than they were for Emerson. First, while slavery in the nineteenth century may have been "an exceptional phenomenon, an aberrant system of atrocity, the political events of this century—beginning with World War One—have established atrocity as the norm."[28] Unlike Emerson's one indignation in relation to slavery, we may be justified in being permanently indignant. Second, moral and practical commitment toward addressing such massive suffering now almost always implies involvement in a relatively organized and orchestrated public campaign. The political machine has multiplied exponentially in size and complexity since Emerson's time, meaning it is difficult for individual involvement to remain individualized. In short, the tensions between mental and active self-reliance, between individuality and democracy appear to have reached crisis point from the Emersonian point of view.

There are dangers in making a choice one way or the other. Kateb is inclined to speak up in favor of the Emersonian ideal and alert us to the risks involved in becoming too politically active. To a sensitive person, the only responsible form of living may seem to have political activism as a central feature. One has to be careful, though, to understand the inner needs and forces that attract us to that particular response to the recognition of evil. Kateb discusses these issues by drawing a contrast between what he calls "deliberate" and "unconscious" aestheticism.[29] For him, the aesthetic is a dominant force in human life. There is a pervasive demand for the kind of beauty, sublimity, and meaningfulness we often find in art. But this desire for the aesthetic can become a dangerous "craving" when it is directed at the social and political world of human affairs. In Kateb's view, "unaware and unrationalized aestheticism" is responsible for a great deal of immorality.[30] More significantly, it represents an "innocent assault on morality" because it is the by-product of noble aspirations.[31] Aesthetic cravings, he says, "can never find gratifications in artworks . . . but inevitably will seek satisfaction in nearly all social phenomena"[32] and this is why we are often able to ignore moral limits that in other circumstances would strike us with great force.

Deliberate aestheticism, however, can be a friend of morality. In this respect, Kateb defines the "aesthetic" in terms of relevant attitudes and feelings as follows:

> Aesthetic *attitudes* are perception, observation, and contemplation; noticing and watching, staring and looking hard; studying and waiting; taking things in and letting nothing be lost; staying with the thing or condition, dwelling with or near it; caring about it while letting it be; and so on. These attitudes arouse or are aroused by essentially aesthetic *feelings*—appreciation; admiration; sometimes wonder, amazement, or astonishment.[33]

In contrast to aesthetic cravings, deliberate aestheticism involves self-control, detachment and distance, allowing things to remain "external to oneself and to affect oneself on their own terms." The work of cultivation involved here leads to a "mitigation of aesthetic cravings" and is "a training for living a less crazy life," "the beginning of a more sane relation to social reality."[34]

Once again, Kateb is concerned with the difference between the active and the passive. And for him, democratic ideals play a central role in distinguishing between the two. On the one hand, aesthetic *cravings* are active, aimed at making the world over into a beautiful scene that then solicits aesthetic feelings and attitudes. *Deliberate* aestheticism, on the other hand, is passive and aims to find beauty in what already exists. It is easy, in Kateb's view, for deliberate cultivation to slip over into craving, thus making aestheticism indifferent to morality: "The tendency to get carried away aesthetically is irrepressible. We are always restlessly seeking to find anywhere in society what we expect to be given . . . by artworks, nature, and designated aesthetic activities and objects."[35] Democratic ideals, however, indicate a method for relating aestheticism to morality in a way that is cooperative rather than hostile. *Democratic* aestheticism contains an inbuilt moral dimension because it accords equal respect to the entire range of things and beings in the world:

> The mission is to make the unpromising world worthy of attention; to grant standing to what seems not to merit it; and to hear the often

> silent or distorted appeal of everyone and everything for perception, interpretation, and contemplation, and hence for some sort of appreciation, if admiration must be withheld.[36]

Democratic aestheticism links the passive quality of aesthetic appreciation with morality because it is a search for beauty within the world as it is, not an attempt to restructure the world in order to then reflect beauty.

Kateb manages to formulate a cooperative relationship between morality and aesthetics. He is still troubled by doubts, though, in a world where it seems impossible not to think some things should be otherwise. For "democratic aestheticism calls for personal reform. . . . By doing that, it dulls the urge to change the world, it leaves the world alone because the world is sufficient as it is. It could thus settle for remaining passive in the face of the very evil that helped to instigate its existence."[37] Once again, the conflict between the moral and the aesthetic, between democracy and individuality reappears just when cooperation was evident. If the very possibility of democratic individuality depends on constitutional governance, are individuals not obligated to be politically involved in sustaining the conditions of possibility of their sense of self? On the other hand, repaying one's debt in this way could be counterproductive. Democratic individuality involves a mistrust of government and a concern to limit its activities. Political participation may well add to the power of organized politics and the importance of the state to daily existence rather than preserve *liberal* democratic institutions.

Kateb insists that the aesthetics of individuality are incompatible with the structures of politics and political involvement. Two different universes of experience are involved here. Individuality moves in the cultural atmosphere of democratic politics rather than in politics itself. Thus, the citizenship "most congenial" to the Emersonians was "participation by lecturing and writing." A "modern equivalent," from Kateb's perspective, "would perhaps be the episodic citizenship of loosely and temporarily associated individuals" who protest against great wrongs and atrocities.[38] But the dilemmas clearly weigh heavily on his conscience given the contemporary "normality" of great wrongs. And, by extension, these dilemmas must affect precisely those who are interested in the demanding practices of cultivation required for democratic individuality. Kateb asks: "Is there a duty to do one's share in actively perpetuating the indispensable resource of democratic individuality? . . . I do not think that one could plausibly answer Yes. As long as there are countless people willing to take part, there can be no duty to do so, no matter how sharply indebted one felt."[39] Nonetheless, he immediately qualifies this point of view with a Weberian-like ethics of responsibility:

> Yet that is a cold answer. It would be good if people who are inclined toward the fuller realization of . . . democratic individuality . . . were to feel ready to compromise with themselves a bit. . . . If by entering

> political life they enter a world lower than the one they leave, they may not perfect their democratic individuality; they may necessarily act inconsistently with their ideal; they may even hurt themselves with power. But because they enter it reluctantly, they may improve the chances that the political artifice that sustains their individuality will be safer. They can tell themselves that they help sustain what sustains their best.[40]

Kateb's hesitancy about political participation points to what he thinks is the most important, though less visible and more arduous, way of meeting one's obligation: the hard work of cultivation. Individuals who are conscientious enough to discipline themselves to an aesthetic appreciation of the world may not be politically active, but their efforts play an important role in sustaining a democratic culture. Political participation is a particular kind of moral-aesthetic temptation and it has its own benefits both for the people involved and for the population at large. According to Kateb's reflections, however, other parts of the citizenry should feel comfortable in performing a different role that is equally, if not more significant, even though it may not be as well recognized or valued.[41]

While we may need, in current circumstances, to qualify and restrain Emerson's aesthetic appreciation with a stronger moral awareness, Kateb helps to warn us against a moral blackmail that uses the magnitude of suffering as a way of suppressing individualist aspirations. I am very sympathetic to Kateb's conception of the relations between politics, aesthetics and individuality. His work is a reminder of how important detachment from the urge to change is itself integral to the expansion of democracy in the modern world. At the same time, I wonder whether he overestimates the importance of liberal democratic institutions to the kind of individuality he values. The doubt involves not so much his claim that liberal democracy is *indispensable* to individuality, although one could note here that other traditions value the equal dignity of every human being, and other institutions and processes are able to create a consciousness of relativity of social conventions and identities. The doubt is more about the *absence of ambiguity* in Kateb's appreciation of the benefits of liberal democracy. One cannot help think, as White says, that "Kateb presents a view of contemporary American democracy that is too politically self-satisfied."[42] For example, while Kateb talks about how liberal democracies contribute towards the possibility of individuality, he says very little about how they provide an environment conducive to the growth of large-scale inequalities in power and wealth. It seems clear that more is needed besides just liberal democratic institutions for there to be reasonable chances for *everyone* to develop their individuality. In any case, it is this voice of critique to which I would now like to listen before reaching more definitive conclusions about the balance between politics, aesthetics and individuality in the next and final chapter.

Connolly and Nietzsche: Can Arts of the Self Be Political?

William Connolly concurs with the ethical level of Kateb's theorizing but he is at odds with its political minimalism. Ethically, in Connolly's view, Kateb problematizes adequately the conventional model of liberal individualism in which a possessive conception of the self is collectively enforced. Kateb also provides a rich alternative in terms of "democratic individuality." But his "juridical conception of politics tends to downplay the degree of political action, militance, and struggle required to establish space for individuality in a liberal society."[43] Kateb writes, says Connolly, as if the social and political context of the Emersonians still existed. It is doubtful that a private, cultural space was available, even then, to most citizens, a space in which they could cultivate an aesthetic sensibility. Connolly is certain that under present circumstances, pervasive practices of surveillance and normalization have robbed the individual of an extrapolitical arena of existence. For him, only organized political resistance and activism can now create room for individuality in an age dominated by an array of institutional and regulative mechanisms. The "politicization of individuality" means, in fact, that the Katebian view is "not merely a benign perspective that does not go far enough. It is an anachronism that misreads paradigmatic threats to individuality in late-modern society."[44]

This section of the chapter outlines key features of Connolly's conception of the relations between politics, aesthetics and individuality. While Kateb thinks liberal democracy is creative of an individuality that is largely free of direct political obligations, Connolly insists that political involvement is unavoidable for individuals interested in aesthetic concerns. He advocates an "agonistic politics" in which existential issues are incorporated and thematized within political interaction and struggle. In order to evaluate his proposals, I will consider both *why* Connolly thinks such a politicization of existential themes is indispensable to individuality and democracy, and *how* he conceives such themes can be made part of the project of enhancing the democratic elements of liberalism. The central question raised by the analysis concerns whether his notion of "arts of the self" can be politicized in the way he would like.

Connolly has a broad picture in mind of "late modernity" which provides the context for his particular conceptualization of the relationship between individuality and democracy. He believes we have entered a period in which the mode of secular reassurance provided by modern society after the death of God has become riven with contradictions. This general idea has already been discussed in the introductory chapter and in a more detailed fashion in chapter 2. It concerns the breakdown in the belief that individuals can provide meaning to their mortal lives by contributing to the modern, collective project of creating a good society. Connolly refers to three defining characteristics of "late modernity" that have undercut this secular model of reassurance: first, "an intensification of the experience of owing one's life and destiny to world-historical, national, and local-bureaucratic forces"; second, "a decline in the confidence many constituencies have in the probable future to which they find themselves contributing in daily life"; and third, "an even more ominous set of future possibilities that weigh on life in the present."[45] In short, one's everyday activities no longer correspond to a broader, coherent attempt to create a better society. Indeed, if there is a correspondence, there is little reason to believe a *better* society will be created.

The key feature of Connolly's argument for present purposes concerns the way in which these features of late modernity have created pressures for an increasing politicization of the existence of individuals. This contention is, as noted above, the reason why Connolly is suspicious of Kateb's formulation of democratic individuality. The intensification of political regulation has come about because nation-states are compelled to introduce more and more measures of domestic control in order to sustain the secular model of reassurance in a global environment of uncertainty. There is, in Connolly's words, "a widening gap between the power of the most powerful states and the power they would require to be self-governing and self-determining." The continuation of the secular model of reassurance in a world marked by this "globalization of contingency" has grave implications. Its goal is unrealizable given the increasing levels of global interdependency through a "contraction of space and time." The problem is that the "gap between world systematicity and state efficacy" is "treated simply as a deficiency to be rectified" thus making ever more desperate the drive for control and order, and making ever more likely future scenarios of disaster and destruction.[46]

The result is a multiplication of subtle and not-so-subtle forms of domestic control. The lives of individuals are subject to ever higher levels of discipline, control and surveillance in an effort to make institutions run efficiently and smoothly. Standards of responsibility, in particular, are extended continually: "One must now program one's life meticulously to meet a more detailed array of institutional standards of normality and entitlement."[47] And along with this raising of expectations, it becomes more difficult to fit in thus exposing oneself to categorization in terms of "otherness" such as delinquency, dependency, abnormality, credit risk or illness to name but a few. For Connolly, this is the dynamic behind the production of identity and difference in late modernity. And because it is so intensively politicized and institutionalized, there is a stark choice for individuals: "One can either treat one's life as a project, negotiating a path through a finely grained network of institutionally imposed disciplines and requirements, or one can struggle against those disciplines by refusing to treat one's life as a project."[48] In the closing sections of this chapter and in the next chapter, I would like to question Connolly's postulation of this dichotomous choice facing individuals in late modernity. In the meantime, I will consider why he thinks Kateb's aesthetic approach to individuality needs to be extended into the realm of democratic political struggle. For he argues that "[i]n a world of closely woven interdependencies, distance must be generated by political means if it is to be at all."[49]

To comprehend the significance of what Connolly terms "arts of the self" is to become aware of the central quality of modern life inhibiting an extension of democratic possibilities: "generalized resentment." Resentment has become pervasive due to the "dependent uncertainty" individuals experience when their lives become subject to intensive practices of discipline and regulation. People are forced to conform to arrangements which, given the global dynamics of contingency, may easily change or become redundant. The emotional life of individuals is completely destabilized in late modernity as they are turned into dispensable appendages of a disordered social machine.

> Dependent uncertainty fosters a character type whose explicit consent to its way of life is laced with generalized resentment. The reactive attitudes of gratitude and resentment are intimately linked already in personal life, as Nietzsche knew. If you are grateful to me for my help, you know that I know you were recently in a position of need or vulnerability. You can easily become resentful over actual or imagined misuses I might make of this knowledge.[50]

At a collective level, especially when personal life is increasingly swamped by collective determinations, this logic of resentment becomes a potent, antidemocratic force. Resentment begins to taint social and political transactions generally but "it receives its most revealing and politically active expression" in the anger directed by the included against the already excluded and underprivileged.[51] When these latter individuals and groups complain about their position, particularly as "beneficiaries" of the modern welfare state, they are likely to become the target of resentment by those who are paying and, moreover, struggling to pay. "What gives these 'others' the right to complain," Connolly asks rhetorically, "when many struggling to measure up to the demands of life as a project already face as much self-discipline, dependency, and uncertainty as they can handle?"[52] "Normal citizens," laboring to contain their resentment and to fit into the demands of everyday, politicized life, find a chance to express and release their resentment when they see others who appear only to take from and not contribute to the conventional, irrational lifestyle. It may even appear, to those who are striving to conform to standards that might shift or become obsolete at any time, that the outsiders have an easier life.

How is it possible, then, to ease the violent pressures of generalized resentment? Connolly believes that a politicization of Nietzsche's insights about overcoming resentment is essential to think about the possibilities for the now interdependent projects of democracy and individuality. Following Nietzsche, Connolly "anchors" his political theory in a recognition of the pervasiveness of human suffering and an understanding of the typical responses made to it. He observes that resentment exerts a powerful magnetism that attracts sufferers to raise the question of responsibility and blame in relation to their distress. Individuals and groups tend to establish their identities and reach conclusions about the world by converting difference into otherness, by contrasting the basis in truth or morality of their selfhood with the inherently evil or irrational identities of others. The propensity for identity to be constructed in this way means violence and conflict of various kinds often dominate social and political life. Connolly believes that since "implication in a particular sort of identity" is both necessary and desirable for human beings, it is crucial we understand better and worse ways of experiencing identity.[53] It is important to find approaches to living identity that avoid and resist the alluring logic of exclusion and domination. He is interested, in particular, in "the arts of experimental detachment of the self from the identity installed within it" that make room for a way of life that recognizes identity is without secure foundations and that cultivate an ethics of care for ambiguity.[54]

Arts of the self are a potential antidote to resentment because they replace the problematic of justification, which tends to be motivated by bitterness at the uncertainty of life, with one of cultivation. Such arts focus on the "tactics" and "techniques" of identity construction always already in existence in order to experiment with alternative methods of relating to oneself and others. Consider, for example, the way such arts might develop responses to the question of death and the political struggles surrounding this question. Connolly argues the importance of our approach to death does not arise simply when the ending of physical life becomes the object of one's attention in one way or another. Rather, our understanding of death, conditioned as it is by metaphysical and religious speculation, structures our everyday existence. Without needing to conduct an empirical survey, we can see that many people are attached to life and fear death. This mentality about life and death expresses a deep-seated wish for continuity. Naturally, it seems, we hope for stability and a chance to realize our potential and the various life-projects we have adopted. This "tenacity of life," says Connolly, is what "impels us towards philosophies of permanence in god, nature, or reason."[55] We convert our *wish* for eternity into a *dogmatic insistence* on the truth of eternity and thus our approach to death can be a potential source of intolerance for the finite structure of life. It is in reflecting on this connection between our view of death and our more mundane attitudes that we expose the techniques of self-construction going on under our noses. We reveal "a fervency for life, a fervency already flowing through one's daily thoughts, actions, routines, decisions, struggles, and successes, a fervency inscribed in the fibers of the body."[56] It is at this point, says

Connolly, that arts of the self have the potential to modify the subtle mechanisms governing the body politic and relieve those pressures for certainty at the roots of political violence.

> The idea might be that by refiguring your own relation to death you are more likely to live without being overtaken by resentment against finitude, to live without projecting a fundamental unfairness into being and then resent "it" for being unfair. . . . You may be more likely to see that part of the demand for a true identity for oneself and others flows from the demand to attain a self-reassurance deep enough to fend off the vicissitudes of life.[57]

Attending to one's relationship with death, then, can have significant implications for how one lives. It may even expand the scope for generosity in one's relations with those others who tend to undermine the stability of one's sense of being.[58]

Connolly admits that all of this talk "may sound like mumbo jumbo"[59] to secularists who think we need to get beyond religious, metaphysical, and existential questions in order to understand how to organize a more democratic society. But secularists, for him, actually sustain the tradition of Christian theism that has greatly diminished our capacity and imagination for being sensitive about difference. It is now relatively easy to see that figures like Augustine "depoliticize[d] issues of identity and responsibility."[60] They exploited hopes and anxieties surrounding the uncertainty and injustice of the human condition so as to entrench their authority and power with promises about stability and universality. They held out, says Connolly, "the transcendental gun" against any who would contest their understanding of the universe.[61] They closed off the possibility of a freer, less fearful, and more humane society in the name of such a society. And yet a similar economy of threats and promises has been continued rather than overcome by a great deal of secular and progressive thought. Many radical democrats have argued politics needs to be limited and contained if pluralism and tolerance are to become features of modern, civic life. Habermas, for example, develops a theory of communicative action designed to set out the normative perimeters within which discourse can safely orbit. And not unlike his Christian predecessors, Habermas raises the specter of a "hangman's noose"—the performative self-contradiction—as a prohibition on the objections of skeptical protagonists.[62]

Connolly believes it is precisely this attempt to establish limits to politics and identity that feeds the dynamic of violence. He hopes to make clear that even though progressive thought presents its limits as harmless and virtuous, these limits are just as debilitating as their more draconian Christian precursors. To call for unity in the context of fragmentation is merely to strengthen the metaphysical resolve of the contending parties. The need is not to modify fragmentation with an abstract synthesis but to prevent "a fixing and consolidation of a set of contending identities, each of which takes itself to be the true identity deserving hegemony." The problem concerns "wrong ways of living identity, not . . . the absence of individual and common identities."[63] The entire attempt to create a center is part of the problem:

> For it may be unnecessary to democratic politics either to establish a *single moral source* around which all other positions rotate, or to create *a public discourse of neutrality* in which all parties shield their metaphysical faiths from public space. The first drive fosters cultural war between dogmatic contenders seeking to occupy the authoritative center. And the second is an academic experiment that has failed philosophically and practically.[64]

Connolly contends the secular model of reassurance is counterproductive because it ignores and even fosters the underlying currents of resentment and stinginess that inhibit democratic politics. It neglects what he calls the "visceral register of subjectivity and intersubjectivity"[65] on which arts of the self do their work. The "visceral" register or dimension of existence is made up of a mixture of biological and cultural forces that subsist at a semiconscious and unconscious level. It involves sensibilities, attitudes and predispositions that are both a source of, and limit to, our reflective capacity for thought and action. The visceral register provides motivation and energy for daily activities as well as circumscribing those activities within boundaries that are sometimes difficult to detect and shift. In figuring our relation to death and the whole host of existential questions confronting human beings, the visceral register is a major determinant of how public institutions operate.

The problem with secularism, says Connolly, is that it screens off these deeper layers of everyday existence from political contestation, even while political contestation itself is heavily influenced by visceral factors. Significantly, our ethical sensibilities and attitudes depend in many ways on a variety of metaphysical and theological assumptions and yet secularism refuses to allow such issues a legitimate voice in public discussion. Connolly believes it is important that arts of the self, which aim to renovate the visceral layers of being, be introduced into democratic contexts by thematizing the metaphysical assumptions of all protagonists in public debate. He thinks this is especially crucial at a time when secularism is in decline and there are vigorous attempts to reenchant the world in a fundamentalist way. Connolly acknowledges this is a "risky enterprise" but it is, in his view, no more dangerous than a secularist approach that ignores its own mode of violence and suppression.

> Today, the need is to draw a larger plurality of metaphysical/religious orientations into public life than heretofore, and to do so in ways that

> encourage more people to adjust more positively to the inevitable bouts of uncertainty, disruption, and surprise to which their own faiths are periodically subjected. For a positive ethos of public life requires more constituencies to respond graciously and generously to elements of comparative contestability in their own religious, secular, and asecular faiths.[66]

I find Connolly's account to be persuasive. I can only agree that the politics of resentment will be impossible to budge unless some of that ballast holding us back from a more generous encounter with difference is reconfigured and made a little lighter. It is, though, a ballast made up of a potent mix of biological, psychological, and cultural elements. And as dangerous as it is to leave this mixture bubbling away beneath the surface of secular politics, I suffer a physical resistance to the suggestion that we bring it all out into the distorting and manipulating light of politics. No doubt this is a visceral reaction prompted by a series of metaphysical and empirical assumptions that I need to contest and perhaps modify. But can arts of the self *really* be politicized?

To examine Connolly's work further in relation to this question it may be useful to probe in more detail his encounter with Nietzsche. Connolly draws inspiration from Nietzsche in order not to shy away from the aftereffects of knowledge, from a bringing out of prejudices and illusions that were previously hidden and untouched. But Connolly does not follow Nietzsche in other ways and he carefully draws the lines along which he cultivates "agonistic respect" with the gay scientist. Nietzsche had an "aristocratic" consciousness of how dangerous his work was, of how he would probably be misinterpreted, and how, of those who did understand, few would be interested in embarking on the remote, dangerous path of politicizing their existence as well. Who really wants to live alone, as he put it, in the "ice and high mountains?" Nietzsche recommended that it is better to deliberately limit politics and build a fund of sacred values and ideals in which most individuals can live in certainty and security, saved from the risks of knowledge and of a politicized life. Connolly, however, believes we now have little choice: politics *is* virtually everywhere, we had better get used to it, and attempts to resist doubt and questioning will merely exacerbate tendencies toward fundamentalism and violence. He argues we should take up the aesthetic opportunities that Nietzsche clarified for us but do so by going beyond Nietzsche, by leaving Zarathustra in his loneliness and by democratizing the *übermensch*. Is this progressive update of Nietzsche really possible? Connolly provides two main reasons for his view that it is both possible and compelling. After considering these reasons, I would like to draw out how some of Nietzsche's reservations creep back into Connolly's account.

First, Connolly claims Nietzsche's concept of the *übermensch* can be preserved only by retrieving it from the tradition of elitism. Nietzsche tended to set apart for the few the possibility of living difference peacefully. He located individuality in a solitary social space separate from mundane political concerns. As one might guess from the above reflections, Connolly maintains "a century of social intensification" has destroyed the conditions of possibility of this conception.[67] He refers to the dense network and web of relations and interdependencies that characterize contemporary life and which make "overcoming" in the sense of social detachment impossible. Because one's identity is so bound up with the dynamics and mechanisms of social reproduction, one has no choice but to either "accept those identifications or to struggle against them politically."[68] No one person can reach a point above and beyond complex practices of discipline and regulation because there is an "intensive entanglement of everyone with everyone else."[69] Connolly thinks these insights are not immobilizing but a spur for reinterpreting the very idea of the *übermensch*. The concept of the *übermensch* is to be withdrawn from an identification with select individuals and located within "a set of dispositions that may compete for presence in any self."[70] "The *distinction between types*," argues Connolly, "now gives way to *struggle within and between selves*."[71] The struggle is primarily one between *ressentiment* and an affirmation of life that accepts difference, and it is a struggle to be engaged publicly and democratically.

Second, Connolly contends that we can use Nietzsche's exaggerated critique of democracy to strengthen democratic politics. Nietzsche claimed progressive culture is self-poisoning due to its sustenance of revengeful attitudes. Democratic radicalism ends up rooting out that gratitude for life required for an ethics of care for difference because it always wants the world to be otherwise and "better." Connolly maintains Nietzsche's sensitivity to *ressentiment* as an element of progressive struggle is a useful reminder. It alerts us to the natural level of human existence beneath the accretion of social and political structures by keeping in mind the fact that not all suffering is socially created and therefore susceptible to elimination. Thus, insofar as democrats and social critics rail against institutions as if the human being is purely social, we can be sure that *ressentiment* is playing a role here. An exclusive focus on the inadequacies of institutions, says Connolly, means the democratic left risks becoming stuck in a "generic cynicism" that "undercuts the nerve of critical action." "It may be wise," he suggests, "to cultivate little spaces of enchantment, both individually and collectively, partly for your own sake and partly to lend energy to political struggles against unnecessary suffering."[72] But insofar as critics like Nietzsche ignore social sources of suffering, we may also be justified in detecting an element of stinginess, an unwillingness to acknowledge *unnecessary* forms of injustice and inequality. The point is that both perspectives have a validity, and the dangers attending a one-sided application of either can be addressed, even if they cannot be avoided, by looking through both. Connolly thinks it might be possible to develop a political theory and practice that "simultaneously refuses to reduce suffering to defects in the structure of society *and* opposes injustices in the distribution of burdens, dangers, and sacrifices imposed by the prevailing order of things."[73] Such a mode of theory and practice would protect democratic politics from inbuilt tendencies toward "generic cynicism."

This is Connolly's rationale, then, for a progressive Nietzscheanism. It is a compelling account, emphasizing the metaphorical quality of many of Nietzsche's pronouncements, and not allowing the exaggerations and hyperbole to form the core around which interpretation is to take place. But Nietzsche's rejection of the political and public possibilities for arts of the self does not go entirely unnoticed. A rejection in Nietzsche turns into a significant reservation in Connolly's work, albeit a reservation he tends to place at the periphery of his reflections. Connolly recognizes, in other words, that there may be a series of important social and economic *conditions of possibility* of his agonistic conception of democracy. He admits, in particular, that a number of inequalities must be considerably minimized if all citizens are to have realistic and desirable opportunities for the kind of political participation he advocates.[74] The world will need to be significantly "better" than it is now if people are to be released from the inward and outward pressures that prevent a free-spirited engagement of identity and difference. For the time being, the violent structural dynamics of politics, economics, and culture constitute an environment too toxic for the growth of "left Nietzschean" sensitivities and subtleties. This environment makes dangerous a contestation of conventional identities, a recognition of the deep contingencies of life, and public discussion about the differences between socially and existentially induced suffering. Without appropriate social and economic conditions, such public debate

> could too readily be received as yet another attack on those already excluded from democratic politics. In the actual world . . . these themes are to be given a modulated expression, one that takes pains to counter misuses some would make of them as they allow a laudatory concern for social justice to screen out the elemental issue of existential resentment.[75]

Connolly appears to open the door here precisely to the kind of logic Habermas uses in his justifications for limiting the scope of democratic politics. Habermas, after all, is well aware of how easily Nietzschean-inspired arguments have been used in the history of modern Germany to buttress a fascist politics. His judgment might be that it is simply too difficult to have a reasonable discussion about the complex causes of suffering and injustice in public life. It is better, considering the dangers involved, to make political calculations about audience reactions and impose limits on the acceptable range of topics available for discussion.

To be sure, Connolly only hesitates at the extension of democracy with these considerations rather than giving up on his argument: the themes he is interested in are to be given a "modulated expression" and not used recklessly. But one may ask more insistently about dismissing Nietzsche's grave doubts regarding democracy given that the required conditions of relative equality still seem to be some way off. Is the average individual, conditioned through and through to experience identity in a resentful way, simply unprepared or unwilling to exercise the skepticism required for arts of the self? Practices of self-cultivation are, after all, an arduous affair requiring considerable hard work. Will the politicization of these arts not add to their complexity for the already overtaxed citizens of late-modern life? And what about those individuals who, for some reason, already have an intimation of that sense of freedom and gratitude that comes from being less attached to identity? Will they, as people genuinely interested in further cultivating care for difference, be prepared to enter the rocky terrain of contemporary public life and seek to engage these issues? Or would it not be wiser for them to practise arts of the self in the relative safety of more privatized, even if regulated, domains? These questions about the relationship between politics, aesthetics, and individuality will be confronted one last time in the next and final chapter, where Connolly's work is examined further.

6

Spaces for Individuality

Can the strains of democracy evident within contemporary liberal orders be strengthened? Positive responses to this question have been considered in the previous two chapters. The "deliberative" and "existential" strategies of democratic expansion set out contrasting trajectories for politics and individuality. They establish different conceptions of the relationship between political processes, on the one hand, and relatively individualized practices of aesthetic cultivation, on the other hand. The argument presented thus far has been that an existential approach better appreciates the important role of individuality in efforts to expand democracy. The proceduralism of Habermas's deliberative orientation, by contrast, represents an attempt to avoid the question of individuality altogether. Its bias toward consensus also works against an aesthetic appreciation of life. The cultivation of such an aesthetic understanding, as claimed throughout this book, is central to individuality and is a key source of progressive change. Nevertheless, existentially oriented theories have their own problems in resolving what appear to be the competing demands of such forms of individuality and democratic politics. The divergent understandings of Kateb and Connolly illustrate some of the tensions and difficulties. While both of these theorists agree that democracy needs the cultivation of individuality, they disagree about the extent of individuals' political obligations. This chapter reaches more definitive conclusions about these issues. The basic claim underlying the arguments put forward is that the "return to ourselves" ensuing from the aftereffects of knowledge cannot and should not be enlisted directly by a political project of extending democracy.

The chapter begins with a critique of Connolly's work. Connolly's approach is, as noted earlier, part of a broader stream of thinking in political theory that goes under the rubric of "agonistic democracy." It is claimed that the agonistic bearing, by recruiting practices of cultivation for political purposes, adds to rather than subtracts from the pressures working against the formation of individuality in the contemporary world. The aesthetic requirements of individuality are, that is, in contradiction with the demands of identity politics. The second section then elaborates on the logic of individuality once it is freed from these kinds of political compulsion. Here it is argued that the development of individuality leads away from the democratic enthusiasm that might be said to characterize the work of theorists such as Connolly.

The third section of the chapter sets out a different understanding of the relationship between individuality and political participation. It puts forward the idea that arts of the self are best mobilized as a mode of *preparing* individuals for engagement with politics as opposed to being made part of the substance and content of political interaction as such. Here, reference is made to Max Weber's reflections on politics as a vocation in order to flesh out this suggestion. A study by Ian Hunter of the emergence of liberal tolerance in early modern Europe is also examined so as to consider an historical example of the kind of political individuality at stake. The key argument reiterated here is that aesthetic cultivation is required for individuals to gain a degree of freedom from themselves. Such freedom is essential if they are to see things from a less self-interested point of view and form a connection with the general and the common, as integral elements of politics.

The fourth section of the chapter brings together some concluding thoughts about the meaning of and relationship between politics, aesthetics, and individuality. It is contended that there are good reasons for developing a certain degree of pessimism about the potential of politics. When we keep in check our enthusiasm about democratic possibilities, politics is protected from overly ambitious expectations that are unsuited to its structural dynamics. Such an approach need not represent an argument against the "radicalization" of democracy. Rather, it suggests that democratic progress must occur indirectly, as indicated by Kateb's analysis. A moderate pessimism preserves spaces for individuality against the compulsions of direct political involvement and makes room for a form of democratic citizenship able to sustain the values of aesthetic appreciation.

Adding to the Pressures Against Individuality

William Connolly argues we gain an appropriate understanding of both morality and politics when we abandon the philosophical problematic of justification. We do not need transcendental guarantees in order to act morally. Rather, freedom from compulsions to vindicate is a condition of possibility of ethics. Likewise, political pluralism does not need to be contained within the apparent safety and security of a common identity, however abstract. On the contrary, democratic forms of interaction are facilitated and enhanced once contending identities no longer attempt to establish a connection with some kind of universalism. For Connolly, this abandonment of justificatory discourse and its accompanying sensibilities is the key to enlivening democratic politics. The hypocrisy of a liberalism that represses metaphysical and religious themes from political life can be overcome by the cultivation of a "generous ethos of engagement." *Contra* procedural liberalism, the potential for violence accompanying the introduction of identity into politics dissipates when the participants aim to come to terms with, rather than transcend, their sense of contingency in relation to one another.

I would like to contend, however, that while Connolly seems to open up this space for individuality, the consequences of the logic governing his work are such as to take this space away. The "light-minded aestheticism," to use Rorty's phrase, ensuing from Connolly's release of those psychological pressures of justification, ends up being radically circumscribed. These other restrictions on individuality derive from his diagnosis of the living conditions and structural dynamics characterizing western societies. That is, restrictions based on his empirical estimation of the pressures facing each individual along with the tremendous problems and dangers thrown up by the workings of modern societies as a whole. As noted in the previous chapter, Connolly claims, first, that individuals are increasingly enmeshed in inhibiting institutional regulations and disciplines and, second, that the refusal of nation-states to respond to the "globalization of contingency" generates greater and greater risks of catastrophe.

My sense is that Connolly's diagnosis of the condition of late modernity has a considerable deal of truth to it. The concern here, though, is with the way he tends to use this diagnosis to *force* through the validity of his arguments about the relations between politics and individuality. Habermas may well be guilty of using a "transcendental gun" to blackmail theoretical opponents into a stark choice between his own position and the stigma of irrationality. But Connolly sometimes has recourse to a gun also, although of a more empirical kind. He argues, in particular, that individuals now face, in light of an accelerated process of politicization, a very difficult decision: "One can *either* treat one's life as a project, negotiating a path through a finely grained network of institutionally imposed disciplines and requirements, *or* one can struggle against those disciplines by refusing to treat one's life as a project."[1] The choice is *either* resign and give in *or* contribute to a political struggle.

In the present context of resentment along with liberal inhibitions about exercising virtues like critical responsiveness, there is little room for different kinds of identity or ways of being. This room to move, insists Connolly, needs to be *politically* created. He emphasizes that "[i]dentities are always collective and relational." "[T]o *become* something new," he says,

> is to *move* the self-recognition and relational standards of judgment endorsed by other constituencies to whom you are connected. . . . Hegemonic identities depend on existing definitions of difference to be. To alter your recognition of difference, therefore, is to revise your own terms of self-recognition as well. . . . In that sense critical responsiveness is always political.[2]

The question is, nevertheless, will a democratic agonism, an explicit introduction of identity into the political arena serve to alleviate the pressures of resentment and create more room for otherness? Or will such an orientation, as liberals have traditionally argued, only exacerbate the conflicts endemic within human life by linking them with a *political* form of contestation? The dichotomy posed by Connolly's radical choice appears valid given that freedom is indeed constricted by high degrees of political surveillance. In my view, though, he presses this choice too hard, excluding all possibilities other than his version of agonistic politics.

Foremost in Connolly's mind, with regard to the advantages and disadvantages of different political strategies, are the dangers attending attempts to keep politics free of existential concerns. He is well aware of the risks associated with his own version of democratic agonism but, for him, they are risks worth taking and they are *explicit* risks, ones that can be consciously considered. Efforts to keep politics "pure," on the other hand, hide their own metaphysical orientations and, in so doing, nurture dangers that cannot be confronted and addressed. Connolly takes Hannah Arendt to task on this point.[3] Not unlike procedural liberals, he claims, Arendt's distinction between the social and the political, as a way of keeping the realm of "necessity" out of the political sphere of "freedom," ignores important conditions of possibility of her own, desired form of political engagement. She ignores the body, in particular, because she assumes its needs and demands are fixed and must necessarily interfere with a politics designed to take place in a "public realm" free of such exigencies. For Connolly, this "political purism" neglects the importance of arts of the self in cultivating the dispositions Arendt herself would like to see characterize political interaction. And arts of the self are crucial because bodily needs and the organization of the "household" are *not* fixed; they are malleable and susceptible to aesthetic considerations. Thus, politics cannot ignore the body or the social question or the host of other contingencies that can be and need to be worked on if it is to become more generous and less resentful. It is necessary, says Connolly, to overcome the visceral resistance to impurity characterizing Arendt's theory in order to advance her own practical aims.

Nonetheless, as alluded to in the previous chapter, there is a certain recognition of the need for purity in politics in Connolly's own work, an acknowledgment that parallels Arendt's understanding of the conditions of possibility of agonistic politics. Connolly admits, as we have seen, that social and economic inequality would need to be reduced substantially if the introduction of metaphysical and religious themes into politics is not to add fuel to the already raging fires of resentment. "The problem," he notes, "is that the ethos of plurality and the politics of economic inclusion each set conditions of possibility for the other; neither advances very far until the other makes progress."[4] Given that inequality is actually increasing rather than diminishing in Western countries, is it then wise to encourage an agonistic politics? If identities enter the political arena in the context of insecurity and scarcity, will they not harden and press their needs in belligerent ways rather than be prepared to cultivate an appreciation of their contingency? Even if there is no choice but to act politically in order to create space for individuality, will individuality not end up being a casualty of this kind of political action, action undertaken out of a deep level of need and necessity? Connolly's encouragement of agonistic politics, in other words, is very likely to add to the considerable pressures already ranged against the cultivation of individuality. It is his binding together of agonistic political action with the creation of space for individuality that I would like to contest.

To take Connolly to task over this it will be useful to explore the thought of Arendt a little further. Connolly is far from alone in wishing to appropriate many of Arendt's insights about politics while trying to detach these insights from other elements of her writing, particularly her distinction between the social and the political. This distinction connotes ideas of exclusion, ideology, and repression since it appears to reserve public spaces only for privileged groups that are freed from the pressures of everyday, material life by the labor of other groups. Any attempt to expand democracy in radical ways cannot accept such a distinction. Still, there may be something quite instructive we can take from this distinction, a lesson that gives us pause to think about the desirability of agonistic politics. Dana Villa salvages this lesson in a way that reminds one of how Connolly sympathetically rewrites Nietzsche's distinction between types of individuals into a distinction between dispositions within all selves.[5] Just as Connolly sees a radical egalitarianism lying within Nietzsche's writing, Villa thinks Arendt's formulations can be read in a similar way by attending to their metaphorical in contrast to their literal and concrete meaning. Villa argues that

> Arendt's distinctions between the social and the political, or the public and the private, are not motivated by a Nietzschean desire to keep the healthy, active few separate from the "sick," resentful masses; nor are they designed to erect a "nonnegotiable" barrier that confines and emasculates her account of "disruptive" action. Rather, these distinctions . . . serve to focus attention on the central role that impersonality and self-distance play in the preservation of a (genuinely) agonistic ethos. What matters for her is less *where* political action takes place and *what* it concerns than the spirit in which it is undertaken.[6]

Villa focuses here on the central feature of individuality as it has been discussed in this book: the sense of detachment from oneself in aesthetic forms of perception. Impersonality, self-distance, a measure of autonomy from one's underlying fears and desires also marks Connolly's description of arts of the self. There is an agreement here that freedom from oneself is essential. But how this freedom can be achieved in relation to politics is in dispute.

Villa's point is that agonistic politics cannot and should not aim to create space for individuality since this form of politics *presumes* such individuality. Connolly's own "purism" in relation to questions such as economic inequality is a recognition of this insight but he does not follow through its implications in a systematic way. I agree with Villa that it is fatal to a serious agonistic politics to include within it struggles for social justice and for the recognition of identity:

> One cannot value the "play of the game" if winning the game is crucial to the sheer survival of oneself or one's group; nor can one value this play of perspectives if the question of basic material subsistence looms larger than all others. For Arendt, an agonistic politics ends where violence, or the most basic demands of the body, intrude.[7]

Arts of the self aim, in my view, to create freedom from oneself as the precondition of both individuality and politics. Political struggles aiming to create space for justice and identity are governed by a different logic, one that feeds off and adds to pressures against an aesthetic appreciation of life. These projects are too incompatible to be combined in the way envisioned by Connolly.

Individuality Without the Constraints of Intersubjectivity

It is easy *not* to be an individual. As Nietzsche says, "All you are now doing, thinking, desiring, is not you yourself."[8] Cultivating individuality is a complex thing: "If the hare has seven skins, man can slough off seventy times seven and still not be able to say: 'this is really you, this is no longer outer shell.'"[9] In this section of the chapter, I would like to reconnect with some of the themes elaborated in the first part of the book to clarify further why individuality needs to be at a distance from the complications of political struggle. If we bracket out the insistence on politics put forward by Connolly, the dynamics of individuality can be better appreciated and it is possible to see how they lead away, not just from direct political action, but from the dimension of intersubjectivity more generally.

The arguments developed in the first part of this book provided a critique of ideas that emphasize the individual's dependence on structures of intersubjectivity. Theorists such as Habermas and Honneth focus on the intersubjective dimension and draw the conclusion that progressive political struggles should aim to develop expanded forms of recognition and mutual respect. Few could disagree with these general aims but I wonder whether the concentration on intersubjectivity is the right way of going about achieving them. Similarly, Connolly, though far more attentive than contemporary critical theory to the inward dimensions of aesthetic self-cultivation, insists on the relational character of identity and the need to bring these themes into politics. It is this insistence and emphasis, I believe, that leads him to instrumentalize arts of the self for the sake of political ends.

The understanding of individuality developed here follows a different direction. Aesthetic forms of appreciation and cultivation, in my view, involve becoming aware of intersubjective forms of dependence in order to partly free oneself from them. This awareness does not necessarily lead away from politics, as will be argued below, but it does retreat from a form of political contestation in which identity assumes great importance. The choice, *contra* Connolly, is not necessarily between either *accepting* or *struggling against* the ways one's identity is bound up with political dynamics. There is also the possibility of not struggling against one's political identifications while aiming to cultivate a measure of detachment from identity. This choice is about gaining a degree of inner freedom from, rather than participating in, the rather violent dynamics of identity politics. From each individual's point of view, there are great dangers in cultivating publicly a Nietzschean ethos in the absence of robust institutional safeguards. Engagement in experimental arts of the self may, therefore, be just as much, if not more, about *protecting* oneself from politics than changing it.

Connolly reminds us that becoming detached from identity and value commitment is never completely realizable. For him, "partial distantiation is both possible and ethically laudable" but we are always "float[ing], swim[ming] and sink[ing]" in some "pool of normality and abnormality."[10] More significantly, perhaps, even the ideal of critical detachment itself is a certain sort of telos for a way of life. Since it is "impossible to become detached as such," he warns, "it is important to articulate the ideal to which your strategies of critical detachment are attaching you."[11] Connolly performs his theory insofar as he puts forward his own attachment to ontological commitments, such as the idea that "life exceeds identity," in order to frame a commitment to a politics of democratic pluralization. The suggestion put forward here, however, is that the cultivation of critical detachment, when not truncated by the pressures of agonistic politics, tends inherently to be attached to a different, more contemplative ideal. Practices that develop a capacity for aesthetic appreciation are biased, that is, away from the intersubjective dimension.

This point was developed in chapter three in relation to the difference between the first-person and third-person points of view. When we follow the development of individuality charted by Nietzsche and the ancient skeptics, we find that it involves the cultivation of an increasingly "objective" view of the world. Individuality emerges insofar as one is able to leave behind the pressures of intersubjective relationships and associated needs for recognition. This perspective can be elaborated further by considering Nietzsche's formulation of a distinctive relationship between the cognitive, moral, and aesthetic dimensions of rationality and value. His understanding of *aesthetic* cultivation can be read, in this respect, in terms of a deliberate remodeling of the relationship between the *cognitive* and the *moral*. Nietzsche's writings are characterized by an attempt to breakdown our faith in morality in the name of science. He talks about morality as a sphere of principle and conviction, as that force which inhibits a more objective, scientific approach to thought: "What has hitherto been forbidden on principle has never been anything but the truth."[12] Philosophical idealism has lived off these moral prohibitions, providing material on which the human need for conviction can continue to live in an age of doubt. Philosophy in this mode uses morality to construct an ideal world that deprives reality and the senses of their meaning and value. Morality and the moral world-order are useful constructs for individuals unable to live well after learning of the often disheartening truths of science. Moral idealism is suited, in other words, to people who have become despondent and pessimistic at the indifference of the world to human aspirations. Kant is one of Nietzsche's key targets in this regard:

> In the face of nature and history, in the face of the thorough immorality of nature and history, Kant was, like every good German of the old stamp, a pessimist; he believed in morality, not because it is demonstrated in nature and history, but in spite of the fact that nature and history continually contradict it.[13]

But the consistency of Nietzsche's effort to think beyond morality as conviction is itself given form by a "thou shalt." When he asks why he has withdrawn faith in morality, he answers: "Out of morality!"[14] Nietzsche, too, is a "man of conscience" but his conscience is of an "intellectual" rather than of a "moral" kind. Here, a scientific spirit emerges in the form of a particular kind of morality and sense for "cleanliness." What Nietzsche calls "chemistry" in *Human, All Too Human* and "physics" in *The Gay Science* is required so as to develop an intellectual conscience, a "conscience behind your 'conscience.'"[15] Being scientific is also about being more philosophical, seeking out the reasons that motivate one's thoughts and actions rather than simply relying on the conventional moral explanations one has received from others. Nietzsche defines science in terms of the "art of self-observation:"

> How many people know how to observe something? Of the few who do, how many observe themselves? . . . Your judgment "this is right"

> has a pre-history in your own instincts, likes, dislikes, experiences, and lack of experiences. "How did it originate there?" you must ask, and then also: "What is it that impels me to listen to it?"[16]

If one disciplines oneself in this art of self-observation, one becomes an immoralist according to conventional standards. Yet Nietzsche also thinks of himself as a great moralist. In his view, science cooperates with a nonconventional understanding of morality whose aim is an inward condition of freedom and happiness. Individuals unable to cope with the "reality" of the world *believe* in a morality in opposition to the world but they do not *live* this morality. A morality made up of beliefs is merely the expression of resentful instincts. Unable to *be* independent and self-reliant, the majority hold a morality made up of timid herd values to be the true and only one. Nietzsche hopes to belong to a different moral community, a community of free spirits in which morality and science go together to form a distinctive kind of virtuous disposition: "Those moralists . . . who, following in the footsteps of Socrates, offer the *individual* a morality of self-control and temperance as a means to his own *advantage*, as his personal key to happiness, *are the exceptions*."[17]

Here, moral ideals are not believed in as much as practised in order to form a certain disposition toward oneself and the world. Also, moral principles emerge from scientific investigation itself. Through a more objective and impartial form of observation, one finds there are good reasons to control and sublimate the feelings of anger, resentment, pity, and injustice that are bound up with the dimension of intersubjectivity. That is, it is to one's physiological and psychological benefit that certain moral codes be adopted.

Connolly's more philosophically oriented work also leads in this direction. He draws, in particular, on recent neuroscientific research in order to elaborate on what Nietzsche already knew long ago, that "[w]e think with our stomachs."[18] Neuroscience helps us become aware of the deep-seated dependence of our conscious life on subterranean forces and opens us up more readily to the importance of techniques and arts of the self. Further to this, the scientific treatment of ourselves as objects in nature enables us to see more clearly how we are merely organisms in which thinking occurs. Emphasis on the first-person perspective, on the other hand, tends to give a false autonomy to conscious thought and the sphere of morality, culture, and relations with others in general. While philosophy done in the first person makes for a "conception of morality set in a supersensible realm,"[19] philosophy undertaken in the third-person is more likely to lead to a form of naturalism. Connolly elaborates what he calls "immanent naturalism," an approach that *naturalizes* the presuppositions of thought as opposed to the Kantian strategy of *transcendentalizing* them.

As argued above, Connolly takes only a few steps toward the third-person view and therefore the development of individuality: he stops and then retreats a little as a result of the demands of agonistic politics. He reintroduces the intersubjective exigencies of the first-person perspective by overvaluing the dimension of identity. In my view, we need to question rather than endorse what appears to be an increasing dependence on others for recognition and identity. It may be that identity politics is perceived to be important and necessary only because it feeds on this dependence. An individuality freed from these kinds of political constraint is able to develop in the direction of greater objectivity, self-distance, and impersonality. These are the ideals that Villa retrieves from Arendt and it is to the role of such ideals in political participation that I would now like to turn.

Individuality and Participation in Politics

Connolly would like to bring into the sphere of political contestation an awareness of the contingency of identity. That implies an introduction of religious and metaphysical themes, although it is not really about "introducing" such themes since they are always already there. The point is to make their presence more obvious and aim to cope with their potential explosiveness by broaching the question of their relativity. Connolly hopes to reconstitute politics with what I believe should only be a *preparation* for political action, a preparation that takes place outside of the space of politics. If political space is to be concerned with issues of public and general significance, as I think it should be, then individuals engaging in political interaction need to have gained some measure of control over their "all-too-human" illusions and weaknesses, especially the need for reassurance. A degree of self-cultivation is an essential prerequisite for being able to perceive issues from the point of view of their public significance in contrast to their relationship to oneself. This section of the chapter elaborates briefly on the meaning and nature of this kind of participation by the individual in politics. It makes an initial reference to Max Weber's well-known remarks on "politics as a vocation." Weber specifies a mode of "political individuality" which, it is argued, draws heavily on the kind of aesthetic considerations which theorists such as Connolly have done so much to advance. Attention then turns to what is considered to be an historical example of this kind of individual involvement in politics, as manifest in the development of statist liberalism in early modern Europe.

For Max Weber, the serious political theorist must keep firmly in view the close connection in the modern world between politics and the state apparatus. Individuals prepared to engage in politics should be clear about how this connection necessarily makes their enterprise a morally ambiguous one, for "the state is a relation of men dominating men, a relation supported by means of legitimate (i.e., considered to be legitimate) violence."[20] Given that violence is the definitive means of politics, there can be no seamless continuum as we move from the ethical to the political spheres. The actor who wishes to graduate from the former domain to the latter is exposed to all kinds of paradoxes and moral difficulties.

> Whoever wants to engage in politics at all, and especially politics as a vocation, has to realize these ethical paradoxes. . . . I repeat, he lets himself in for the diabolic forces lurking in all violence. . . . He who seeks the salvation of the soul, of his own and of others, should not seek it along the avenue of politics, for the quite different tasks of politics can only be solved by violence.[21]

To paraphrase Weber in the terms set out in this book: whoever is interested in developing individuality by cultivating an aesthetic appreciation of the world should think more than twice about becoming politically active.

Weber does not mean that politics is completely divorced from ethical and aesthetic concerns. On the contrary, his ideal-typical political actor is motivated by "ultimate values." One of the "three pre-eminent qualities . . . decisive for the politician" is "passion," in the sense of "passionate devotion to a 'cause,' to the god or demon who is its overlord."[22] But the factor of passion needs to be complemented by two other elements, "a feeling of responsibility" and "a sense of proportion." These three features combine, for Weber, into an "ethic of responsibility" that takes into account the consequences of action as distinguished from an "ethic of ultimate ends" which has regard only for intentions.[23] He believes that the politician's devotion to a cause should be moderated once she enters the political arena. If the cause is to be served "objectively," then the politician must strive after and make use of power without being consumed by it. Weber heaps scorn on the "power politician" who abandons her cause and seeks only the feeling of power. Such an individual displays a "shoddy and superficially blasé attitude towards the meaning of human conduct" and possesses very little understanding of the "knowledge of tragedy with which all action, but especially political action, is truly interwoven."[24] On the other hand, to enter politics without passion is equally contemptible and "the curse of the creature's worthlessness overshadows even the externally strongest political successes."[25] Weber claims there is a need for a mutual relationship between "warm passion and a cool sense of proportion . . . in one and the same soul."[26]

Weber's ethic of responsibility, as a restraint on one's ultimate values, is something like Connolly's ideal of folding generosity and forbearance into the enlivening but potentially violent energy of one's identity. Of course, the two differ in many ways, one important difference relating to how the conduct of practices of self-cultivation should relate to political action. Significantly, Weber indicates that arts of the self have an important albeit *indirect* political relevance: such arts form an essential *preparation* for the kind of action which, in his view, is distinctively political. In this connection, he speaks of "the decisive psychological quality of the politician" being "his ability to let realities work on him with inner concentration and calmness. Hence his distance to things and men."[27] "[W]hat is decisive is the trained relentlessness in viewing the realities of life, and the ability to face such realities and to measure up to them inwardly," to possess a "degree of inner poise."[28] Without these *inward* characteristics, political actors contribute to the corruption of the political with the acid of their personal weaknesses. To decide whether an individual has a calling for politics, we need only see if their commitment to a cause survives a deep knowledge of the tragic quality of political action. Weber argues the individual who engages in politics without fully realizing what is involved will, over time, sink into one of three essentially antipolitical states of mind: cynicism, dull conformity or "mystic flight from reality."[29]

Much else of what Weber has to say about politics, such as his desire for a plebiscitary leader, can be detached from these insights about the preparation required by individuals for political participation. A similar approach, I believe, can be adopted in the case of Connolly whose valuable contribution to our understanding of arts of the self need not be intrinsically tied to the project of an agonistic identity politics. Drawing on elements of both theorists, the argument here is that a sounder connection between the methodology of individuality and the meaning of political action is one where individuals earn the right to see things from a relatively general and impersonal point of view, and therefore the right to see what is genuinely *political*. An example of this kind of political individuality can be found in the conflicts surrounding the formation of the liberal state in early modern Europe. I would now like to turn to this historical instance of the involvement of individuality in politics so as to build on the above reflections.

Ian Hunter has sought to retrieve a form of "rival enlightenment" that has often been suppressed in intellectual histories about the initial formation of the liberal state. This process of suppression has been made possible by the adoption of a particular philosophical view, one that sees history as a dialectical process. This view, promulgated by "university metaphysicians" such as Kant, Leibniz, and Wolff, was meant to explain the transcendent and otherworldly basis of the modern liberal state. These philosophers, according to Hunter, sought to provide a rational successor to the Christian culture in which political authority is justified with reference to an overarching order of things. He argues that because of the success and dominance of this interpretation of enlightenment down to our time, we have been unable to recognize properly a rival enlightenment. This competitor has been ignored because it has been understood falsely, in the terms set out by the philosophical discourse of the university metaphysicians. Hunter aims to resuscitate this tradition and, in so doing, adds to the Weberian understanding of the relationship between philosophy and political action.

For the rival group of "civil philosophers," claims Hunter, the state neither can nor should be grounded in any kind of otherworldly, metaphysical or universal moral basis. It must be "grounded," in their view, in the systematic cultivation by political actors of an indifference toward such philosophical concerns for the sake of purely worldly and civil desires such as peace and security. Philosophy, from this perspective, becomes sectarian as soon as it seeks any "higher" justification of the state and politics. Hunter explains that this exclusion of truth and symbolic concerns meant a "recalibration of politics and law as instrumental disciplines whose object was restricted to political order as such."[30] This did not amount to an instrumentalization of all social spheres. On the contrary, it was directed specifically toward the political and legal levels, leaving religion as a private matter divorced from worldly authority.[31] However, and this is the significant point in this context, civil philosophy still drew on metaphysical resources in its project. In addressing jurists and stateswomen, as expert cultures charged with civil power, it painted an "Epicurean" conception of the human, of a "passion-driven self-destructive being"[32] with a "limitless capacity for mutual self-destruction."[33] These metaphysical resources were not designed to justify political authority, but meant to form part of an art of self-cultivation in which political actors learned to "take up a particular relation to themselves and their world."[34]

Metaphysical philosophy, naturally, was shocked at this "indifference of sovereign power to moral truth" and the "autonomy of the political" and sought to relink politics and philosophy in terms of the problematic of justification.[35] Contrary to their own self-understanding, though, Hunter insists these metaphysicians were engaged in a purely secular conflict over access to political power, prestige, and influence.

> It was Kant who showed moral philosophers how to re-enter the domain of political governance from which they had been expelled. They would return not as a clerical estate possessing its own share of civil authority, but as a clerisy of academic intellectuals, claiming powers from a source higher than the end of social peace—"critical reason."[36]

Kant engaged in this conflict with impressive philosophical symbols, developing a "transcendent conception of good and evil, designed to outflank the civil determination of ethics in terms of man's worldly need for peace and security."[37] Here, too, says Hunter, we can think of the link between politics and philosophy in terms of the self-cultivation of significant actors, although this particular link meets with his disapproval. That is, Kantian metaphysics, built up around a division of the world into the phenomenal and noumenal, effectively trains individuals to adopt a higher rationality, divorced from empirical considerations and designed to guide the political process along normative lines. As Hunter notes, Kant's philosophy is "surely a modern form of . . . Platonic exercises in 'mental concentration and renunciation of the sensible world.'"[38] The problem with this philosophy, however, is that it sees itself differently and is therefore ignorant of its actual political implications.

Politics Without Meaning and Individuality as Citizenship

Hunter outlines, in my view, an historical instance of the kind of individuality which is necessary for distinctively *political* action. It is a mode of individuality in which metaphysical considerations and aesthetic practices of cultivation are meant to groom the self for political participation rather than form the content of political interaction as such. This understanding of the relations between politics and individuality preserves both from significant dangers. It protects politics from being overwhelmed by the explosive conflicts contained within metaphysical disputes and it shields individuality from being distorted by political pressures. This section of the chapter concludes the book with a final elaboration of the implications of this approach for the relations between politics, aesthetics, and individuality. It considers, in particular, the type of citizenship most appropriate to a gradual expansion of our democratic capacities.

There is a value in being pessimistic about politics. The early modern statist liberals, as well as Connolly, subscribe to a kind of Epicurean "pessimism" about the human condition as a whole in contrast to a rationalistic view characterized by hopes for historical progress. But while this pessimism motivates the liberals to separate politics from aesthetic concerns in an effort to put a lid on conflictual egoism, it leads Connolly to try and demonstrate that the potential for human strife can be democratically and politically engaged rather than suppressed. Connolly's "pessimism" stops short of politics. If we consistently think through the implications of the loss of metaphysical meaning in history, however, I cannot see how we can still link questions of meaning directly with the political realm. Without the progressive assumptions analysed in chapter 2, politics must lose its connection with human aspirations for fulfilment and self-realization, even when such ideals are formulated in "negative" ways. The political then comes to mean a concern with rather mundane, albeit very important, material concerns such as peace and security which, in an age of advanced capitalism, needs to be about more than simply limiting the scope of religion in public life.

A consistent but moderate pessimism clarifies the meaning of politics. Reading Schopenhauer can school one into taking this perspective. Schopenhauer emphasizes that a popular view of life claims that pleasure and happiness are "positive" elements of being whereas pain and suffering are "negative" in character. For him, the actual state of affairs is the reverse, since suffering is the normal condition while happiness presents itself on rare occasions and lasts only briefly. Happiness is better understood as a kind of void or emptiness, existing only in the absence of the positive element of suffering. For Schopenhauer, both the pervasiveness of suffering and the way it makes us more aware of our existence suggests its "positivity": "We are conscious not of the healthiness of our whole body but only of the little place where the shoe pinches."[39] Without our willfulness and the resistance to it—frustration, obstruction, pain, difficulties, struggle—we would dwell within a trouble-free consciousness. The volitional drive of human beings means, though, that there is a relentless tendency to leave and move away from this negative realm into the domain of striving and all the emotional travails that go with it. Thus, while the individual often says he hopes to find peace, he *actually*, and mostly unconsciously, seeks out strife and fills his life with turbulence through the mere fact of living: "He discovers adversaries everywhere, lives in continual conflict and dies with sword in hand."[40]

Schopenhauer emphasizes the *intersubjective* dynamics of human conflict. If we compare human beings with the rest of the animal kingdom, for example, we find that while all share the same material ground of existence, they differ markedly in their *experience* of physical pleasure and pain. Essentially, both are happy or frustrated according to "health, food, protection from wet and cold, and sexual gratification; or the lack of these things."[41] Nonetheless, with a capacity for reason, thought, and memory, human beings raise the stakes of seeking pleasure and avoiding pain. Beyond and apart from *actual* satisfaction and dissatisfaction in the purely physical sense, humans develop fears and anticipations, cares and hopes, an extra layer of concern with the realization of basic needs. Without this capacity to build such a complex psyche, the animal is far less affected by the *desire for* pleasure and the *fear of* pain and possesses an "enviable composure and unconcern."[42] Even more important, the element of reflection in human life creates a source of pleasure and suffering that comes to control and direct all the rest: one's conception of one's relationships with others. For each individual, this involves "ambition and the sense of honor and shame—in plain words, what he thinks others think of him."[43]

Once again, these insights are useful reminders to make us sober when we begin to think about politics and perhaps get carried away with transferring "positive" ideals onto the political realm. Such reminders also point to the importance of freeing politics from an exaggerated emphasis on intersubjectivity and connecting it with ideals of impersonality and self-distance. Since, in Schopenhauer's view, justice is a negative concept and cannot be defined, it is both foolish and irresponsible to advocate a political order which sanctions the pursuit of something that only fuels willfulness. Because "*injustice* is the order of the day," it is clear the state can exist only for purposes of protection.[44] Schopenhauer thinks a pessimistically based ethics located in private spheres, meanwhile, might serve to ease the pressures which make for political strife.

He recommends the practise of definite values, such as patience, humility, forgiveness, and tolerance. If we recognize that suffering is built into our existence and that we almost "deserve" it because of the mere fact of being alive, we can also ease and temper the emotions that intensify our sensitivity to pleasure and pain. But if we insist on thinking we have a right to happiness, that this state is positive and therefore an object of striving, we will merely aggravate our suffering and deepen the more or less nascent conflicts and hostilities in our relationships. Schopenhauer believes that because we are bound to inflict suffering on ourselves and others through multiple vanities and anxieties, it is better to accept this human condition and moderate its intensity rather than continue, in a foolish way, to seek out ever more desperately and violently what is unattainable.

As claimed earlier, such a perspective is not only protective of the political, it also preserves spaces for individuality. Nietzsche's "dionysian" approach to pessimism is, I believe, superior to Schopenhauer's perspective in regard to ethics but the general point remains: The recruitment of individuality by projects like agonistic democracy contradict the cultivation of an aesthetic appreciation of life and place an inappropriate burden on the political realm. To allow individuality to develop free of such participatory political projects may seem to be irresponsible in an age where regard for public goods is at an all-time low. Carefree forms of individuality appear to compound the privatism and consumerism of contemporary culture and the devaluation of shared interests. It is tempting, in this situation, to become morally committed, cultivate civic virtue and advocate higher levels of political participation. These are the temptations, however, that individuals need to resist if they are to become more aesthetically receptive to life.[45]

To warn against enthusiastic forms of democratic participation is not to deny the importance of democracy and citizenship. It implies, rather, the formulation of a specific account of what citizenship entails and how it can contribute to a more indirect strengthening of democracy. As Villa argues, lack of moral and political commitment is not necessarily the contemporary problem. Attempts are made constantly to capture hearts and minds for the sake of a cause. There is, perhaps, a surplus of commitment in modern life. Rarer is the ability to put commitment at a distance, to wear gloves in the presence of ideals as Nietzsche puts it. Villa defends what he calls "Socratic citizenship" that "is not the quest for either a meaningful common good or a 'noble' form of life but rather the constant reminder that *all* such conceptions can be incitements to injustice, and that a minimally moral life consists in the relentless resistance to such incitements."[46] The search for commitment is a sure sign of lack of self-reliance and a willing ally in projects that create injustice in the name of ending it. To be sure, the value of forbearance in political commitment is emphasized in all thoughtful theories of democratic radicalism, but it is not always upheld in a consistent fashion.

The cultivation of individuality, as it has been understood in this book, forms a stronger bulwark against the pressures to conform and jump onto a bandwagon. In this regard, it is important to note that the implications of skepticism, as stated in chapter 3, are not simply negative. Skepticism need not necessarily lead to a sense of emptiness which makes one vulnerable to violent reassertions of meaning. It is also a route to the "positivity" of individuality that is radically different in kind from the positivity of belief. Villa develops this point in defending his Socratic conception of citizenship against the impressive range of "engaged" models to be found in contemporary political theory:

> Skepticism and doubt, together with individualism, are routinely singled out as the corrupting evils of our time, the things which stand in the way of a healthy (and much-needed) civic or moral engagement. The idea that one can be skeptical and morally serious—that a particular form of negativity is crucial to moral seriousness—is dismissed out of hand since moral seriousness is reflexively identified with the passion or conviction with which one pursues a political cause or set of positive moral doctrines.[47]

As set out in the introduction, an insight into the positivity of negativity becomes available when we reorient our approach to knowledge away from a cognitive viewpoint and focus instead on the role of knowledge in the aesthetic formation of the individual. To conceive of citizenship in terms of individuality and of a refusal to be brow-beaten into less thoughtful forms of political participation is to maintain the spirit of *democratic* forms of change. We can only expect a better society to the extent that there are changes in our everyday forms of living, as the soil out of which political systems grow. And change in this area requires, paradoxically, detachment from the pressure to change, namely the cultivation of aesthetic kinds of individuality.

Notes

INTRODUCTION

1. Friedrich Nietzsche, *Human, All Too Human*, trans. Marion Faber and Stephen Lehmann (London: Penguin Books, 1984), "Of First and Last Things," sec. 34.

2. Anthony Giddens, "Brave New World: The New Context of Politics," in *Reinventing the Left*, ed. David Miliband (Cambridge: Polity Press, 1994), p. 22.

3. Wendy Brown, *States of Injury: Power and Freedom in Late Modernity* (Princeton: Princeton University Press, 1995), p. 3.

4. Romand Coles, *Rethinking Generosity: Critical Theory and the Politics of* Caritas (Ithaca: Cornell University Press, 1997), pp. 1–2.

5. Plato, "The Apology" in *The Last Days of Socrates*, trans. Hugh Tredennick and Harold Tarrant (London: Penguin Books, 1993), 32a.

6. F. M. Cornford, *Before and After Socrates* (Cambridge: Cambridge University Press, 1968), p. 28.

7. Plato, *Theaetetus*, trans. John McDowell (Oxford: Clarendon Press, 1973), 150c2.

8. Zygmunt Bauman, *Legislators and Interpreters* (Cambridge: Polity Press, 1987), pp. 119–120.

9. Paul Connerton, *The Tragedy of Enlightenment: An Essay on the Frankfurt School* (Cambridge: Cambridge University Press, 1980), p. 26.

10. Jürgen Habermas, *Moral Consciousness and Communicative Action* (Cambridge: Polity Press, 1990), p. 1.

11. Max Horkheimer, "Traditional and Critical Theory," in *Critical Theory: Selected Essays*, trans. Matthew O'Connell, et al. (New York: Herder and Herder, 1972).

12. Seyla Benhabib, *Critique, Norm and Utopia* (New York: Columbia University Press, 1986), p. 4.

13. Jürgen Habermas, *The Philosophical Discourse of Modernity*, trans. Frederick Lawrence (Cambridge: Polity Press, 1987), p. 16.

14. Ibid., p. 51.

15. Ibid., p. 7.

16. Stephen White, *Sustaining Affirmation: The Strengths of Weak Ontology in Political Theory* (Princeton: Princeton University Press, 2000).

17. Ibid., pp. 6–12.

18. Barbara Herrnstein Smith, *Belief and Resistance: Dynamics of Contemporary Intellectual Controversy* (Cambridge: Harvard University Press, 1997), p. 44.

19. Jane Bennett, "'How Is It, Then, That We Still Remain Barbarians?' Foucault, Schiller, and the Aestheticization of Ethics," *Political Theory* 24, no. 4 (1996), p. 656.

20. Ibid., p. 654.

21. See, for example, Julia Annas, *The Morality of Happiness* (Oxford: Oxford University Press, 1993); Pierre Hadot, *Philosophy as a Way of Life: Spiritual Exercises from Socrates to Foucault*, trans. Michael Chase (Oxford: Blackwell, 1995) and Martha Nussbaum, *The Therapy of Desire: Theory and Practice in Hellenistic Ethics* (Princeton: Princeton University Press, 1994).

22. Alexander Nehamas, *The Art of Living: Socratic Reflections from Plato to Foucault* (Berkeley: University of California Press, 1998). Nehamas talks about an "inward turn" on p. 131.

23. Ian Hunter, *Rival Enlightenments: Civil and Metaphysical Philosophy in Early Modern Germany* (Cambridge: Cambridge University Press, 2001).

24. See also Ian Hunter, "Metaphysics as a Way of Life," *Economy and Society* 23, no. 1 (1994).

25. Hunter, *Rival Enlightenments*, p. 21.

26. Ibid., p. 23.

27. Ibid., pp. 21–22

28. Jürgen Habermas, *The Theory of Communicative Action, Volume One: Reason and the Rationalization of Society* (Cambridge: Polity Press, 1984), pp. 43–74.

29. Ibid., p. 240.

30. Habermas recognizes that concepts such as "rationalization" and "learning processes" cannot be uniformly applied across the three dimensions of rationality, particularly with regard to the aesthetic sphere. And yet he insists on the rationalization problematic as a framework of understanding. See, for example, Jürgen Habermas, "Questions and Counterquestions," in *Habermas and Modernity*, ed. Richard Bernstein (Cambridge: Polity Press, 1985), p. 207.

31. Coles, *Rethinking Generosity*, p. 141.

32. Ibid., p. 170.

33. Ibid., p. 167.

34. Martin Morris, *Rethinking the Communicative Turn: Adorno, Habermas and the Problem of Communicative Freedom* (New York: State University of New York Press, 2001), p. 7.

35. Roland Bleiker, "The Aesthetic Turn in International Political Theory," *Millennium* 30, no. 3 (2001), p. 510.

36. Morton Schoolman, *Reason and Horror: Critical Theory, Democracy, and Aesthetic Individuality* (New York: Routledge, 2001), p. 4.

37. See, for example, Jacinda Swanson, "Self Help: Clinton, Blair and the Politics of Personal Responsibility," *Radical Philosophy* 101, May/June (2000).

38. Richard Rorty, *Objectivity, Relativism, and Truth: Philosophical Papers, Volume 1* (Cambridge: Cambridge University Press, 1991), p. 207.

39. Ibid., p. 12.

40. Ibid., p. 2.

41. Ibid., p. 13.

42. Richard Rorty, *Contingency, Irony and Solidarity* (Cambridge: Cambridge University Press, 1991), p. 63.

43. Rorty, *Objectivity, Relativism and Truth*, p. 15.

44. Ibid., p. 13.

45. Rorty, *Contingency, Irony and Solidarity*, p. 65.

46. Ibid., p. xiv.

47. Ibid., p. 65.

48. Rorty, *Objectivity, Relativism, and Truth*, p. 190.

49. William Connolly, "Review Symposium on Richard Rorty," *History of the Human Sciences* 3, no. 1 (1990), p. 105.

50. Ibid.

51. Ibid., p. 104.

52. Ibid., p. 107.

53. William Connolly, *Identity\Difference. Democratic Negotiations of Political Paradox* (Ithaca: Cornell University Press, 1991), p. 190.

54. Bonnie Honig, *Political Theory and the Displacement of Politics* (Ithaca: Cornell University Press, 1993), p. 201.

55. Thomas McCarthy, *The Critical Theory of Jürgen Habermas* (Cambridge: Polity Press, 1984), p. ix.

Chapter 1

1. See, for example, Seyla Benhabib, *Critique, Norm and Utopia* (New York: Columbia University Press, 1986) and Thomas McCarthy, "Practical Discourse: On the Relation of Morality to Politics," in *Habermas and the Public Sphere*, ed. Craig Calhoun (Cambridge: MIT Press, 1992).

2. See, for example, Hans Joas, "The Unhappy Marriage of Hermeneutics and Functionalism," and Thomas McCarthy, "Complexity and Democracy: Or the Seducements of Systems Theory," both in *Communicative Action: Essays on Jürgen Habermas's* The Theory of Communicative Action, eds Axel Honneth and Hans Joas (Cambridge: Polity Press, 1991).

3. Axel Honneth, *The Critique of Power: Reflective Stages in a Critical Theory*, trans. Kenneth Baynes (Cambridge: MIT Press, 1991) and *The Struggle for Recognition*, trans. Joel Anderson (Cambridge: Polity Press, 1995).

4. The distinction between "validity claims" and "identity claims" will be discussed further in the third section of the chapter.

5. Aristotle, *Nicomachean Ethics*, trans. J. A. K. Thomson (London: Penguin Books, 1976), 1105a9–b2.

6. NE 1172a19–b1.

7. NE 1105b2–1106a20.

8. NE 1176a30–1176b13.

9. Plato, *The Laws*, trans. Trevor J. Saunders (London: Penguin Books, 1970), 646–650.

10. Plato, *The Laws*, 644.

11. See, for example, NE 1103b1–25 and Plato, *The Republic*, trans. Desmond Lee (London: Penguin Books, 1987), 401–403.

12. NE 1179b7–29.

13. Julia Annas, *The Morality of Happiness* (Oxford: Oxford University Press, 1993).

14. Jürgen Habermas, *Theory and Practice*, trans. John Viertel (London: Heinemann, 1974), chapter 1.

15. Ibid., p. 43.

16. Habermas's mature "theory of communicative action" includes an estimation of the appropriate balance between complexity and democracy in modern societies.

17. Jürgen Habermas, *Toward a Rational Society*, trans. Jeremy Shapiro (London: Heinemann, 1971), p. 56.

18. Habermas, *Theory and Practice*, p. 44.

19. Jürgen Habermas, *Between Facts and Norms: Contributions to a Discourse Theory of Law and Democracy*, trans. William Rehg (Cambridge: Polity Press, 1996), p. 22.

20. Jürgen Habermas, "A Reply," in *Communicative Action: Essays on Jürgen Habermas'ss* The Theory of Communicative Action, eds Axel Honneth and Hans Joas, trans. Jeremy Gaines and Doris Jones (Cambridge: Polity Press, 1991), p. 252.

21. Jürgen Habermas, *The Theory of Communicative Action, Volume One: Reason and the Rationalization of Society*, trans. Thomas McCarthy (Cambridge: Polity Press, 1984), pp. 144–145, 270–271, 343; *The Theory of Communicative Action, Volume Two: The Critique of Functionalist Reason*, trans. Thomas McCarthy (Cambridge: Polity Press, 1987), pp. 113ff, 303–306. Up until *The Theory of Communicative Action*, Habermas had failed to make this point clear.

22. Habermas, *Theory of Communicative Action, Volume Two*, p. 202. Earlier in his career, Habermas had maintained exactly the opposite: see *Theory and Practice*, p. 205.

23. Ibid., p. 339.

24. Jürgen Habermas, "A Reply to My Critics," trans. Thomas McCarthy, in *Habermas: Critical Debates*, eds J. Thompson and D. Held (London: Macmillan, 1982), p. 223.

25. Jürgen Habermas, "Further Reflections on the Public Sphere," trans. Thomas Burger, in *Habermas and the Public Sphere*, ed. Craig Calhoun (Cambridge: MIT Press, 1992), p. 444.

26. See, for example, Dieter Misgeld, "Critical Hermeneutics versus Neoparsonianism?" *New German Critique* 35 (1985).

27. See Habermas, "A Reply," pp. 254, 257.

28. Barbara Herrnstein Smith, *Belief and Resistance: Dynamics of Contemporary Intellectual Controversy* (Cambridge: Harvard University Press, 1997), p. 112.

29. Ibid., p. 112.

30. McCarthy, "Complexity and Democracy," p. 166.

31. Ibid., p. 168.

32. See, for example, Nancy Fraser, "What's Critical about Critical Theory?" in *Feminism as Critique*, eds Seyla Benhabib and Drucilla Cornell (Cambridge: Polity Press, 1987) and Jeff Livesay, "Habermas, Narcissism, and Status," *Telos* 64 (1985).

33. James Bohman, "Formal Pragmatics and Social Criticism: The Philosophy of Language and the Critique of Ideology in Habermas'ss *Theory of Communicative Action*," *Philosophy and Social Criticism* 11 (1986).

34. McCarthy, "Complexity and Democracy," pp. 177–178.

35. Seyla Benhabib, *Critique, Norm and Utopia*, pp. 330–331.

36. Cited in Thomas McCarthy, *The Critical Theory of Jürgen Habermas* (Cambridge: Polity Press, 1984), p. 334.

37. See, especially, the essay "Individuation through Socialization: on George Herbert Mead's Theory of Subjectivity," in Jürgen Habermas *Postmetaphysical Thinking*, trans. William Mark Hohengarten (Cambridge: Polity Press, 1992).

38. Ibid., pp. 177–178.

39. Jürgen Habermas, *Moral Consciousness and Communicative Action* (Cambridge: Polity Press, 1990), p. 199.

40. Ibid.

41. Consider, for example, Habermas's reflections on suicide, *Moral Consciousness and Communicative Action*, p. 200 and Jürgen Habermas, *The Philosophical Discourse of Modernity*, trans. Frederick Lawrence (Cambridge: Polity Press, 1987), p. 316.

42. Jürgen Habermas, *Knowledge and Human Interests*, trans. Jeremy Shapiro (Boston: Beacon Press, 1971), p. 56. See also *Theory and Practice*, p. 148 and *Philosophical Discourse of Modernity*, pp. 28–29.

43. Habermas, *Knowledge and Human Interests*, p. 56.

44. See Martin Jay, "The Debate over Performative Contradiction: Habermas versus the Poststructuralists," in *Philosophical Interventions in the Unfinished Project of Enlightenment*, eds. Axel Honneth, et al. (Cambridge: MIT Press, 1992).

45. Habermas, *Postmetaphysical Thinking*, p. 190.

46. Dieter Freundlieb, "Rethinking Critical Theory: Weaknesses and New Directions," *Constellations* 7, no. 1 (2000), p. 86.

47. Habermas, *Philosophical Discourse of Modernity*, p. 29.

48. Habermas, *Postmetaphysical Thinking*, p. 183.

49. Habermas, *Philosophical Discourse of Modernity*, p. 301 and *Postmetaphysical Thinking*, p. 25.

50. Habermas, *Philosophical Discourse of Modernity*, p. 296.

51. For a brief overview of the debate and a "resolution" in favor of an intersubjectivity different in kind from Habermas's see David Stern, "The Return of the Subject? Power, Reflexivity and Agency," *Philosophy and Social Criticism* 26, no. 5 (2000).

52. Peter Dews, "The Paradigm Shift to Communication and the Question of Subjectivity: Reflections on Habermas, Lacan and Mead," *Revue Internationale de Philosophie* 194 (1995), p. 519.

53. As Dews notes, Habermas appears to admit this in talking about the continuing relevance of religious language: ibid., p. 518.

54. Joel Whitebook, "Intersubjectivity and the Monadic Core of the Psyche: Habermas and Castoriadis on the Unconscious," *Praxis International* 9 (1990), p. 358.

55. Jürgen Habermas, "Further Reflections on the Public Sphere," trans. Thomas Burger, in *Habermas and the Public Sphere*, ed. Craig Calhoun (Cambridge: MIT Press, 1992), p. 442.

56. Habermas, *Between Facts and Norms*, p. 341. These themes will be discussed further in chapter 4.

57. Michele Mangini, "Character and Well-Being: Towards an Ethics of Character," *Philosophy and Social Criticism* 26 (2000), p. 83. These issues will be examined in more detail in the second part of the book.

58. NE 1103b26–1104a11.

59. See Jürgen Habermas, *Communication and the Evolution of Society*, trans. Thomas McCarthy (Boston: Beacon Press, 1979), p. 164.

60. Habermas, "A Reply to my Critics," pp. 222–223.

61. Nancy Fraser, "From Redistribution to Recognition? Dilemmas of Justice in a 'Post-Socialist' Age," *New Left Review* 212 (1995).

62. Ibid., p. 91.

63. Mangini, "Character and Well-Being," p. 88.

64. Honneth, *The Struggle for Recognition*, p. 172.

65. Ibid., p. 69.

66. Ibid., p. 132.

67. Ibid., p. 136.

68. Ibid., p. 174.

69. Dieter Henrich, "What Is Metaphysics—What Is Modernity? Twelve Theses Against Jürgen Habermas," in *Habermas: A Critical Reader*, ed. Peter Dews (Oxford: Blackwell, 1999), p. 315.

70. On the ambiguous role of "dissatisfaction" as a normative anchoring point for critical theory, see Freundlieb, "Rethinking Critical Theory," pp. 83–84.

Chapter 2

1. See, for example, Nancy Fraser, "From Redistribution to Recognition? Dilemmas of Justice in a 'Post-Socialist' Age," *New Left Review* 212 (1995).

2. William Connolly, *Why I Am Not a Secularist* (Minneapolis: University of Minnesota Press, 1999), p. 50.

3. Jürgen Habermas, *Legitimation Crisis*, trans. T. McCarthy (Boston: Beacon Press, 1975), p. 78.

4. Julia Annas, *The Morality of Happiness* (Oxford: Oxford University Press, 1993).

5. Arthur Schopenhauer, *Studies in Pessimism*, trans. T. B. Saunders (London: George Allen & Unwin, 1890), p. 33.

6. Jürgen Habermas, "Modernity Versus Postmodernity," trans. Seyla Benhabib, *New German Critique* 22 (1981), p. 9.

7. Karl Löwith, *Meaning in History: The Theological Implications of the Philosophy of History* (Chicago: University of Chicago Press, 1949).

8. G. W. F. Hegel, *The Philosophy of History*, trans. J. Sibree (New York: Dover, 1956).

9. Jürgen Habermas, *The New Conservatism*, trans. Shierry Weber Nicholsen (Cambridge: Polity Press, 1989), p. 51.

10. Jürgen Habermas, *The Philosophical Discourse of Modernity*, trans. Frederick Lawrence (Cambridge: Polity Press, 1987), p. 392, n4.

11. Ibid. See also Jürgen Habermas, *The Theory of Communicative Action, Volume One: Reason and the Rationalization of Society*, trans. Thomas McCarthy (Cambridge: Polity Press, 1984), pp. 145–155.

12. Habermas, *Theory of Communicative Action, Volume One*, p. 15.

13. Cited in ibid., p. 245.

14. Jürgen Habermas, *The Theory of Communicative Action, Volume Two: The Critique of Functionalist Reason*, Thomas McCarthy (Cambridge: Polity Press, 1987), pp. 391–396.

15. Ibid., p. 392.

16. Ibid., p. 393.

17. Ibid., p. 394.

18. Cf. Geoff Dow and George Lafferty, "From Class Analysis to Class Politics: A Critique of Sociological Interpretations of Class," *Australian and New Zealand Journal of Sociology* 26, no. 1 (1990) who argue that the sociological focus of "class analysis" obscures the significance of "class politics," the latter being political conflict over class issues rather than the conscious political activity of classes as agents.

19. Habermas, *Theory of Communicative Action, Volume Two*, p. 391, speaks of "an (unbiased) investigation of tendencies *and* contradictions."

20. Jürgen Habermas, *Knowledge and Human Interests*, trans. Jeremy Shapiro (Boston: Beacon Press, 1971), p. 288.

21. Kenneth Keniston, *Youth and Dissent: The Rise of a New Opposition* (New York: Harcourt Brace Jovanovich, 1971).

22. Ibid., pp. 3, 5.

23. Ibid., p. 6.

24. Ibid., p. 20.

25. Ibid., p. 21.

26. Habermas, *Legitimation Crisis*, pp. 90–92 and *Theory of Communicative Action, Volume Two*, pp. 386–389.

27. Habermas, *Legitimation Crisis*, p. 90.

28. Ibid., p. 75.

29. Erich Fromm, *Escape from Freedom* (New York: Avon, 1968).

30. See, for example, Richard Eckersley, *Casualties of Change: The Predicament of Youth in Australia: An Analysis of the Social and Psychological Problems Faced by Young People in Australia* (Canberra: AGPS [Commission for the Future], 1988).

31. Once again, these claims amount only to an *interpretation*, although an interpretation which has, I believe, considerable support. Both the theoretical understanding of the "adolescent crisis" and the characterization of young people's well-being are disputed. See, for example, the debate between Judith Bessant and Rob Watts, "History, Myth Making and Young People in a Time of Change," *Family Matters* 49 (1998) and Richard Eckersley, "Rising Psychosocial Problems Among Young People: Historical Myth or Contemporary Reality?" *Family Matters* 50 (1998).

32. Lynelle Moon, Paul Meyer, and Jacqueline Grau, *Australia's Young People: Their Health and Well-Being 1999. The First Report on the Health of Young People Aged 12–24 Years by the Australian Institute of Health and Welfare* (Canberra: Australian Institute of Health and Welfare, 1999). A "mental disorder" is defined as "a clinically recognizable set of symptoms or behavior associated in most cases with distress and with interference with personal functions," p. 246.

33. Ibid., p. 34.

34. Ibid., p. 80.

35. Ibid., p. 79. With respect to suicide, an Australian study confirmed that the "recent emphasis and focus on youth suicide is based on a correct diagnosis: youth suicide (ages 15–24) has tripled since the mid-1960s, from around 10 per 100,000 to 30 per 100,000." See Christopher Cantor, Kerryn Neulinger and Diego De Leo, "Australian Suicide Trends 1964–1997: Youth and Beyond?" *The Medical Journal of Australia* 171 (1999). It noted, though, that efforts toward suicide prevention should be extended to include men aged between 25–34 years. There has been no significant increase in the rate of suicide for young women. However, a number of reasons could account for this difference other than a better state of mental health. The much higher incidence of depression in women compared to men is just one consideration.

36. Commonwealth Department of Health and Aged Care and Australian Institute of Health and Welfare, *National Health Priority Areas Report: Mental Health—A Report Focusing on Depression* (Canberra: Barnes Desktopping and Design, 1999), p. 5.

37. Ibid., p. 34. These projections were made by the World Bank and the World Health Organization. The essays collected in David Levin, *Pathologies of the Modern Self: Postmodern Studies on Narcissism, Schizophrenia, and Depression* (New York: New York University Press, 1987) provide a broader theoretical understanding of why depression is a central feature of the "pathologies of the modern self."

38. Eckersley, *Casualties of Change*, pp. 33–39 and Richard Eckersley, "Values and Visions: Youth and the Failure of Modern Western Culture," *Youth Studies Australia* 14, no.1 (1995), pp. 13–14, 17–18.

39. Richard Eckersley, in "Dialogue on Despair: Assessing the West's Cultural Crisis," *The Futurist* 28, no. 2 (1994), p. 20.

40. Richard Eckersley, "Future Visions, Social Realities and Private Lives: Exploring the Links Between How Young People See the Future and Their Personal Well-being," in *Youth Futures: Empirical Research and Transformative Visions*, eds J. Gidley, S. Inayatullah, F. Hutchinson and M. Bussey (Westport, Conn.: Bergin & Garvey, 2001).

41. See Richard Eckersley, *Quality of Life in Australia: An Analysis of Public Perceptions* (Lyneham: The Australia Institute, 1999).

42. Eckersley, in "Dialogue on Despair," p. 20.

43. Löwith, *Meaning in History*, p. 204.

44. Ibid., p. 4.

45. Hannah Arendt, "The Concept of History: Ancient and Modern," in her *Between Past and Future: Six Exercises in Political Thought* (London: Faber and Faber, 1954), p. 80.

46. Max Horkheimer and Theodor Adorno, *Dialectic of Enlightenment*, trans. J. Cumming (London: Allen Lane, 1973), p. 16.

47. Werner Dannhauser, "Nietzsche and Spengler on Progress and Decline," in *History and the Idea of Progress*, eds A. M. Melzer, J. Weinberger and M. R. Zinman (Ithaca: Cornell University Press, 1995), pp. 132–133.

48. Michele Mangini, "Character and Well-being: Towards an Ethics of Character," *Philosophy and Social Criticism* 26 (2000).

49. These considerations relate to contemporary debates in political philosophy about the relationship between the "right" and the "good." The focus on the right by theorists such as Habermas and Rawls stifles the questioning of values on which judgments about justice rest. It means, in the context of a liberal culture and capitalist society, that the protection of rights and the equal distribution of economic resources is most important and thereby assumes and reinforces "narrowly limited views of people as agents interested only in desire-satisfaction": Mangini, "Character and Well-Being," p. 95.

50. Connolly, *Why I Am Not a Secularist*, p. 15.

51. Ibid., p. 16.

52. See also Wendy Brown, *States of Injury: Power and Freedom in Late Modernity* (Princeton: Princeton University Press, 1995).

53. Jane Bennett, *The Enchantment of Modern Life: Attachments, Crossings, and Ethics* (Princeton: Princeton University Press, 2001).

54. Cf. Richard Rorty, *Contingency, Irony, and Solidarity* (Cambridge: Cambridge University Press, 1989), p. 86.

CHAPTER 3

1. Immanuel Kant, *Critique of Pure Reason*, trans. Paul Guyer and Allen W. Wood (Cambridge: Cambridge University Press, 1998), pp. 100–101.

2. Jürgen Habermas, *Justification and Application*, trans. Ciaran Cronin (Cambridge: Polity Press, 1993), p. 22.

3. Plato, *Republic*, trans. Desmond Lee (London: Penguin Books, 1987), 537B–539E.

4. Ibid., 537C.

5. Ibid., 537E.

6. Ibid.

7. Ibid., 538D.

8. Ibid.

9. Ibid., 538D–E.

10. Ibid., 538E.

11. Ibid., 539D.

12. Alasdair MacIntyre, *After Virtue* (London: Duckworth, 1981), p. 118.

13. Bernard Williams, *Ethics and the Limits of Philosophy* (Cambridge: Harvard University Press, 1985), p. 163.

14. Jürgen Habermas, *The Theory of Communicative Action, Volume One: Reason and the Rationalization of Society*, trans. Thomas McCarthy (Cambridge: Polity Press, 1984), pp. 82–83 and *Volume Two: The Critique of Functionalist Reason* (Cambridge: Polity Press, 1987), pp. 77–111.

15. Jürgen Habermas, *The Philosophical Discourse of Modernity*, trans. Frederick Lawrence (Cambridge: Polity Press, 1987), pp. 114ff.

16. Habermas, *Philosophical Discourse of Modernity*, p. 116.

17. Habermas, *Theory of Communicative Action, Volume Two*, p. 353.

18. Habermas, *Philosophical Discourse of Modernity*, p. 119.

19. Jürgen Habermas, *Moral Consciousness and Communicative Action*, trans. Christian Lenhardt and Shierry Weber Nicholsen (Cambridge: Polity Press, 1990), p. 14.

20. Ibid., p. 104.

21. Ibid., p. 99.

22. Ibid.

23. Ibid., p. 98.

24. Jürgen Habermas, *The New Conservatism*, trans. Shierry Weber Nicholsen (Cambridge: Polity Press, 1989), p. 51.

25. Habermas, *Moral Consciousness and Communicative Action*, p. 100.

26. Jürgen Habermas, *Between Facts and Norms: Contributions to a Discourse Theory of Law and Democracy*, trans. William Rehg (Cambridge: Polity Press, 1996), p. 446.

27. Judith Butler, *Gender Trouble: Feminism and the Subversion of Identity* (New York: Routledge, 1990), p. 33.

28. Ibid., p. 30.

29. Ibid., p. 20.

30. Ibid., p. xi.

31. Judith Butler, *Bodies That Matter: On the Discursive Limits of "Sex"* (New York: Routledge, 1993), p. 28.

32. Ibid., p. 10.

33. Butler, *Gender Trouble*, p. 16.

34. Judith Butler, *The Psychic Life of Power: Theories in Subjection* (Stanford: Stanford University Press, 1997), p. 17.

35. Butler, *Bodies That Matter*, p. 15.

36. Butler, *Psychic Life of Power*, pp. 7, 20.

37. Ibid., p. 9.

38. Ibid., p. 12.

39. Ibid., p. 6.

40. Butler, *Bodies That Matter*, p. 220.

41. Butler, *Psychic Life of Power*, p. 12.

42. Alan D. Schrift, "Judith Butler: Une Nouvelle Existentialiste?" *Philosophy Today* Spring 2001.

43. Ibid., p. 21.

44. Stephen White, *Sustaining Affirmation: The Strengths of Weak Ontology in Political Theory* (Princeton: Princeton University Press, 2000). George Kateb, Charles Taylor, and William Connolly are the other three representatives.

45. Ibid., p. 151.

46. Ibid., pp. 151–153

47. Ibid., p. 10.

48. Ibid., p. 11.

49. Ibid.

50. Ibid., p. 103.

51. Friedrich Nietzsche, *Human, All Too Human*, trans. Marion Faber and Stephen Lehmann (London: Penguin Books, 1984), "Preface," sec. 3.

52. Ibid.

53. Friedrich Nietzsche, *The Gay Science*, trans. Walter Kaufman (New York: Vintage, 1974), "Preface for the Second Edition," sec. 4.

54. Nietzsche, *Human All Too Human*, "Preface," sec. 4.

55. Nietzsche, *The Gay Science*, "Book Five," sec. 357.

56. Ibid.

57. Ibid., sec. 346.

58. Friedrich Nietzsche, *Ecce Homo*, trans. R. J. Hollingdale (London: Penguin Books, 1992), "The Birth of Tragedy," sec. 2.

59. Nietzsche, *The Gay Science*, "Book Five," sec. 370.

60. Ibid.

61. Friedrich Nietzsche, *Human, All Too Human*, "Of First and Last Things," sec. 34.

62. Ibid.

63. For accounts of the "Pyrrhonian" conception of tranquillity and happiness leading on from "suspension of judgment," see for example Julia Annas, *The Morality of Happiness* (Oxford: Oxford University Press, 1993), pp. 351–363 and Richard E. Flathman, "The Self Against and for Itself: Montaigne and Sextus Empiricus on Freedom, Discipline and Resistance," *The Monist* 83 (2000), pp. 494–497.

64. See Julia Annas and Jonathan Barnes, *The Modes of Skepticism: Ancient Texts and Modern Interpretations* (Cambridge: Cambridge University Press, 1985) for basic texts of and detailed commentary on the "ten modes."

65. Julia Annas, "Doing Without Objective Values: Ancient and Modern Strategies," in *The Norms of Nature: Studies in Hellenistic Ethics*, eds. Malcolm Schofield and Gisela Striker (Cambridge: Cambridge University Press, 1986), p. 35.

66. Annas, "Doing Without Objective Values," p. 6.

67. Ibid., pp. 9–10, 12–13.

68. Ibid., p. 20.

69. As Flathman, "The Self Against and for Itself," p. 496 notes, "the skeptic trains herself not only to suspend judgment concerning rival doctrines and claims, but to expect and hence to look for considerations that at once oppose and balance one another such that the only appropriate . . . response is to suspend judgment."

70. Annas, "Doing Without Objective Values," pp. 18–23.

71. Ibid., p. 19.

72. Friedrich Nietzsche, *Ecce Homo*, "Foreword," sec. 3.

73. Friedrich Nietzsche, *Twilight of the Idols/The Anti-Christ*, trans. R. J. Hollingdale (London: Penguin Books, 1990), "What the Germans Lack," sec. 6.

74. White, *Sustaining Affirmation*, p. 153.

75. Habermas, *Moral Consciousness and Communicative Action*, p. 105.

76. Butler, *Psychic Life of Power*, p. 29.

77. See, for example, Friedrich Nietzsche, *The Birth of Tragedy*, trans. Shaun Whiteside (London: Penguin Books, 1993) and *On the Genealogy of Morality*, trans. Carol Diethe (Cambridge: Cambridge University Press, 1994).

78. William Connolly's recent work, which draws on interesting developments in neuroscientific research, is especially relevant in thinking about the modes of investigation that might develop within an ontology which sees nature and culture as continuous with one another. See, for example, his "Brain Waves, Transcendental Fields and Techniques of Thought," *Radical Philosophy* March/April, no. 94 (1999).

CHAPTER 4

1. See Friedrich Nietzsche, *Beyond Good and Evil*, trans. R. J. Hollingdale (London: Penguin Books, 1990), "Maxims and Interludes," sec. 146.

2. James Bohman, "The Coming Age of Deliberative Democracy," *The Journal of Political Philosophy* 6, no. 4 (1998), p. 415.

3. Jürgen Habermas, *Between Facts and Norms: Contributions to a Discourse Theory of Law and Democracy*, trans. William Rehg (Cambridge: Polity Press, 1996), p. xlii.

4. Ibid., p. xliii.

5. Jürgen Habermas, *Theory and Practice*, trans. John Viertel (London: Heinemann, 1974), chapter 1.

6. Jürgen Habermas, *The Theory of Communicative Action, Volume One: Reason and the Rationalization of Society* (Cambridge: Polity Press, 1984) and *The Theory of Communicative Action, Volume Two: The Critique of Functionalist Reason* (Cambridge: Polity Press, 1987).

7. Jürgen Habermas, "On the Cognitive Content of Morality," *Proceedings of the Aristotelian Society* 96 (1996), pp. 352–353

8. Habermas, *Between Facts and Norms*, p. 107.

9. Ibid., pp. 118–131.

10. Ibid., p. xli.

11. Ibid., p. 114, emphasis added.

12. Jürgen Habermas, "Postscript (1994)" in his *Between Facts and Norms*, p. 452. Habermas is actually referring here to law rather than procedure, but I would like to argue that the legal is only one aspect of his broader proceduralist approach to compensation.

13. Habermas, *Theory of Communicative Action, Volume Two*, pp. 77–87 and *Between Facts and Norms*, pp. 73–76.

14. Habermas, *Between Facts and Norms*, p. 177.

15. Ibid., pp. 121–123.

16. Ibid., p. 118.

17. Ibid., p. 170.

18. Ibid., pp. 340–341.

19. Immanuel Kant, "What Is Enlightenment?" in his *Foundations of the Metaphysics of Morals and What is Enlightenment?*, trans. Lewis White Beck (Indianapolis: The Bobbs-Merrill Company, 1959), p. 87.

20. Ibid., p. 92.

21. Habermas, *Between Facts and Norms*, p. 116.

22. Friedrich Nietzsche, *Untimely Meditations*, trans. R. J. Hollingdale (Cambridge: Cambridge University Press, 1997).

23. Habermas, *Between Facts and Norms*, p. 114.

24. See, for example, ibid., p. 302.

25. Ibid., p. 307.

26. Ibid., p. 366.

27. Ibid., pp. 379–384.

28. Ibid., pp. 354–356.

29. Ibid., p. 382.

30. Jürgen Habermas, "Reply to Symposium Participants," in *Habermas on Law and Democracy: Critical Exchanges*, eds Michel Rosenfeld and Andrew Arato (Berkeley: University of California Press, 1998), p. 385.

31. Habermas, *Between Facts and Norms*, p. 301.

32. Ibid., pp. 298–302.

33. Ibid., p. 341.

34. Habermas, "Postscript," p. 461.

35. Habermas, *Between Facts and Norms*, p. 119.

36. Ibid., p. 19.

37. Habermas, "Postscript," p. 455.

38. Habermas, *Between Facts and Norms*, pp. 446–447.

39. See, for example, Thomas McCarthy, "Practical Discourse: On the Relation of Morality to Politics," in *Habermas and the Public Sphere*, ed. Craig Calhoun (Cambridge: MIT Press, 1992) and William Rehg and James Bohman, "Discourse and Democracy: The Formal and Informal Bases of Legitimacy in Habermas's *Faktizität und Geltung*," *The Journal of Political Philosophy* 4 (1996).

40. McCarthy, "Practical Discourse," p. 62.

41. See also Jay Bernstein, *Recovering Ethical Life: Jürgen Habermas and the Future of Critical Theory* (London: Routledge, 1995).

42. Habermas, *Between Facts and Norms*, pp. 151–168.

43. Habermas, "Postscript," p. 462.

44. Rehg and Bohman, "Discourse and Democracy," p. 94. These authors reconstruct a weaker set of epistemic conditions for democratic deliberation, pp. 94–99.

45. Jürgen Habermas, *Moral Consciousness and Communicative Action* (Cambridge: Polity Press, 1990), pp. 207–208.

46. McCarthy, "Practical Discourse," pp. 65–69.

47. Ibid., p. 66.

48. On the inadequacy of Habermas's more recent responses to these issues, see Romand Coles, *Rethinking Generosity: Critical Theory and the Politics of* Caritas (Ithaca: Cornell University Press, 1997), pp. 198–200.

49. Mark Warren, "The Self in Discursive Democracy," in *The Cambridge Companion to Habermas*, ed. Stephen White (Cambridge: Cambridge University Press, 1995).

50. Ibid., pp. 168–181.

51. Ibid., pp. 194–195.

52. Warren suggests this is the case when he seeks to carve out a therapeutic dimension in the project of discursive democracy, ibid., pp. 184–193.

53. Ibid., pp. 324–325.

54. Jürgen Habermas, "Individuation Through Socialization: On George Herbert Mead's Theory of Subjectivity," in *Postmetaphysical Thinking*, trans. William Mark Hohengarten (Cambridge: Polity Press, 1992), p. 196.

55. Habermas, *Moral Consciousness and Communicative Action*, p. 199.

56. Habermas, *Theory of Communicative Action, Volume Two*, p. 388. For further elaboration of this issue, see Habermas, "Individuation Through Socialization," pp. 189–190. See also Warren, "The Self in Discursive Democracy," pp. 183–184.

57. Jeff Livesay, "Habermas, Narcissism, and Status," *Telos* 64 (1985).

58. Habermas, *Theory of Communicative Action, Volume One*, pp. 43–74.

59. Jürgen Habermas, *Philosophical-Political Profiles*, trans. Frederick Lawrence (Boston: MIT Press, 1983), p. 158.

60. Cf. Jane Bennett, *The Enchantment of Modern Life: Attachments, Crossings, and Ethics* (Princeton: Princeton University Press, 2001), p. 131.

61. Jürgen Habermas, *Justification and Application*, trans. Ciaran Cronin (Cambridge: Polity Press, 1993), pp. 75–76.

62. Jürgen Habermas, *Legitimation Crisis* (Boston: Beacon Press, 1975), p. 78.

63. Bennett, *The Enchantment of Modern Life*, p. 80.

64. William Connolly, *Identity\Difference. Democratic Negotiations of Political Paradox* (Ithaca: Cornell University Press, 1991), p. 162.

65. Ibid.

66. Ibid.

CHAPTER 5

1. Richard Rorty, "Posties," *London Review of Books* 3 September (1987), p. 12.

2. Richard Rorty, "The Priority of Democracy to Philosophy," in his *Objectivity, Relativism, and Truth: Philosophical Papers, Volume 1* (Cambridge: Cambridge University Press, 1991), p. 182.

3. Ibid., p. 193.

4. Ralph Waldo Emerson, "Self-Reliance," in *Selected Essays*, ed. Larzer Ziff (London: Penguin Books, 1982), p. 178.

5. Ralph Waldo Emerson, "Power," in *The Works of Ralph Waldo Emerson. Volume Two: English Traits, The Conduct of Life, Nature* (London: G. Bell and Sons, 1913), p. 216.

6. Emerson, "Self-Reliance," p. 178.

7. Ralph Waldo Emerson, "Montaigne; or, the Skeptic," in *Selected Essays*, ed. Larzer Ziff (London: Penguin Books, 1982), p. 319.

8. Ibid., p. 320.

9. Friedrich Nietzsche, *Twilight of the Idols/The Anti-Christ*, trans. R. J. Hollingdale (London: Penguin Books, 1990), "What the Germans Lack," sec. 6.

10. Friedrich Nietzsche, *Ecce Homo*, trans. R. J. Hollingdale (London: Penguin Books, 1992), "Foreword," sec. 3.

11. See, generally, George Stack, *Nietzsche and Emerson: An Elective Affinity* (Athens: Ohio University Press, 1992), pp. 268–279, 338–343.

12. Friedrich Nietzsche, *Beyond Good and Evil,* trans. R. J. Hollingdale (London: Penguin Books, 1990), "Our Virtues," sec. 225.

13. Ralph Waldo Emerson, "Politics," in *The Works of Ralph Waldo Emerson. Volume One: Essays and Representative Men* (London: G. Bell and Sons, 1913), p. 307.

14. Stack, *Nietzsche and Emerson*, p. 342.

15. George Kateb, *The Inner Ocean: Individualism and Democratic Culture* (Ithaca: Cornell University Press, 1992), p. 83.

16. Ibid., pp. 84, 85–86.

17. Ibid., p. 25.

18. Ibid., p. 104.

19. Ibid., p. 1.

20. Ibid., p. 7.

21. George Kateb, *Emerson and Self-Reliance* (Sage: Thousand Oaks, 1995), p. xxix.

22. Ibid., p. 4. One is reminded here of a statement by Nietzsche, *Ecce Homo*, "Foreword," sec. 3: "I do not refute ideals, I merely draw on gloves in their presence."

23. Ibid., p. 6.

24. Emerson in ibid., p. 22.

25. Emerson in ibid., p. 27.

26. Ibid., pp. 198, 199.

27. Emerson in ibid., p. 187.

28. Ibid., p. 198.

29. George Kateb, "Aestheticism and Morality: Their Cooperation and Hostility," *Political Theory* 28, no. 1 (2000).

30. Ibid., p. 6.

31. Ibid., p. 19.

32. Ibid.

33. Ibid., p. 21.

34. Ibid., pp. 21, 22.

35. Ibid., p. 23.

36. Ibid., p. 31.

37. Ibid., p. 34.

38. Kateb, *The Inner Ocean*, p. 103.

39. Ibid., p. 105.

40. Ibid. Kateb concludes his study *Emerson and Self-Reliance* with a similar call to perform a difficult balancing act, to hold onto the sense of innocence and beauty required for self-reliance but also not to become heedless of the evil in the world. Since "[s]elf-reliance is the soil and fruit and flower of modern democracy," an "experienced innocence" is needed: Kateb, *Emerson and Self-Reliance*, p. 202.

41. In reflecting on the momentous changes that have reshaped the world of global politics in recent times, Roland Bleiker reminds us of "an approach to social change that focuses less on spectacular revolutionary events and more on the slow transversal transformation of values that precedes them." See his *Popular Dissent, Human Agency and Global Politics* (Cambridge: Cambridge University Press, 2000), pp. 21–22.

42. Stephen White, *Sustaining Affirmation: The Strengths of Weak Ontology in Political Theory* (Princeton: Princeton University Press, 2000), p. 38.

43. William Connolly, *Identity\Difference. Democratic Negotiations of Political Paradox* (Ithaca: Cornell University Press, 1991), p. 81.

44. Ibid., p. 85.

45. Ibid., p. 20.

46. Ibid., p. 24.

47. Ibid., p. 21.

48. Ibid.

49. Ibid., p. xi.

50. Ibid., p. 22.

51. Ibid., p. 23.

52. Ibid.

53. Ibid., p. 9.

54. Ibid.

55. Ibid., p. 168.

56. Ibid., p. 170.

57. Ibid., pp. 164–165.

58. See, for example, Connolly's reflections on the "right to doctor-assisted death" in his *Why I am Not a Secularist* (Minneapolis: University of Minnesota Press, 1999), pp. 146–148.

59. Connolly, *Why I Am Not a Secularist*, p. 28.

60. Connolly, *Identity\Difference*, p. 151.

61. Connolly, *Why I Am Not a Secularist*, p. 137.

62. Ibid., p. 10.

63. Connolly, *Identity\Difference*, p. 172.

64. Ibid., p. 94.

65. Connolly, *Why I Am Not a Secularist*, p. 3.

66. Ibid., p. 15.

67. Connolly, *Identity\Difference*, p. 189.

68. Ibid., pp. 187–188.

69. Ibid., p. 188.

70. Ibid., p. 187. Connolly notes, though, that Nietzsche could have been speaking metaphorically all along and referring merely to different inclinations within everybody.

71. Ibid., p. 189.

72. Connolly, *Why I Am Not a Secularist*, p. 17.

73. Connolly, *Identity\Difference*, p. 191.

74. Ibid., pp. 191–192.

75. Ibid., p. 197.

Chapter 6

1. William Connolly, *Identity\Difference. Democratic Negotiations of Political Paradox* (Ithaca: Cornell University Press, 1991), p. 21, emphasis added.

2. William Connolly, *The Ethos of Pluralization* (Minneapolis: University of Minnesota Press, 1995), p. xvi.

3. William Connolly, *Why I Am Not a Secularist* (Minneapolis: University of Minnesota Press, 1999), p. 177–184.

4. Ibid., p. 186.

5. See the third section of chapter five above.

6. Dana Villa, "Democratizing the Agon: Nietzsche, Arendt, and the Agonistic Tendency in Recent Political Theory," in his *Politics, Philosophy, Terror: Essays on the Thought of Hannah Arendt* (Princeton: Princeton University Press, 1999), pp. 117–118.

7. Ibid., p. 123.

8. Friedrich Nietzsche, *Untimely Meditations*, trans. R. J. Hollingdale (Cambridge: Cambridge University Press, 1997), "Schopenhauer as Educator," sec. 1.

9. Ibid.

10. Connolly, *Ethos of Pluralization*, p. 98.

11. Ibid., p. 35.

12. Friedrich Nietzsche, *Ecce Homo*, trans. R. J. Hollingdale (London: Penguin Books, 1992), "Foreword," sec. 3.

13. Friedrich Nietzsche, *Daybreak: Thoughts on the Prejudices of Morality*, trans. R. J. Hollingdale (Cambridge: Cambridge University Press, 1997), "Preface," sec. 3.

14. Ibid., sec. 4.

15. Friedrich Nietzsche, *The Gay Science*, trans. Walter Kaufman (New York: Vintage, 1974), "Book Four," sec. 335.

16. Ibid.

17. Nietzsche, *Daybreak*, "Book I," sec. 9.

18. Connolly, *Why I Am not a Secularist*, p. 175.

19. William Connolly, "Brain Waves, Transcendental Fields and Techniques of Thought," *Radical Philosophy* March/April, no. 94 (1999), p. 22.

20. Max Weber, "Politics as a Vocation," in *From Max Weber: Essays in Sociology*, trans. H. H. Gerth and C. Wright Mills (London: Routledge, 1991), p. 78.

21. Ibid., pp. 125–126.

22. Ibid., p. 115.

23. Ibid., p. 120.

24. Ibid., p. 117.

25. Ibid.

26. Ibid., p. 115.

27. Ibid.

28. Ibid., p. 127.

29. Ibid., p. 128.

30. Ian Hunter, *Rival Enlightenments: Civil and Metaphysical Philosophy in Early Modern Germany* (Cambridge: Cambridge University Press, 2001), p. 89.

31. Ibid., pp. 89–90.

32. Ibid., p. 27

33. Ibid., p. 89.

34. Ibid., p. 22.

35. Ibid., p. 91.

36. Ibid., p. 265.

37. Ibid., p. 50.

38. Ibid., p. 365.

39. Arthur Schopenhauer, *Essays and Aphorisms*, trans. R. J. Hollingdale (Harmondsworth: Penguin, 1970), p. 41.

40. Ibid., p. 42.

41. Ibid., p. 43.

42. Ibid.

43. Ibid.

44. Ibid., pp. 149, 152–153.

45. See Dana Villa, *Socratic Citizenship* (Princeton: Princeton University Press, 2001).

46. Ibid., p. 58.

47. Ibid., p. xiii.

Index